DAVID O'LEARY - MY STORY

DAVID
O'LEARY
MY STORY

DAVID O'LEARY
WITH
HARRY MILLER

MAINSTREAM
PUBLISHING

Copyright © David O'Leary & Harry Miller, 1988

First published in Great Britain in 1988 by
MAINSTREAM PUBLISHING COMPANY
(EDINBURGH) LTD
7 Albany Street, Edinburgh EH1 3UG

British Library Cataloguing in Publication Data
O'Leary, David
  David O'Leary: my story.
  1. England. Association football. O'Leary,
  David
  I. Title   II. Miller, Harry
  796.334'092'4

  ISBN 1-85158-145-6
  ISBN 1-85158-146-4 Pbk

Typeset in 11½ on 13½ Times by
Blackpool Typesetting Services Ltd., Blackpool.
Printed in Great Britain by Billings & Sons Ltd., Worcester.

DEDICATED TO ARSENAL FOOTBALL CLUB.

I OWE THEM EVERYTHING.

CONTENTS

CHAPTER ONE

Summer of Discontent

Liam Brady was a hero in Italy, Frank Stapleton had just collected an FA Cup winner's medal at Manchester United . . . and I was left asking, "What price loyalty?"

It was Monday, 13 May 1985. An indifferent season for Arsenal had finished 48 hours earlier with a meaningless 2-2 draw at West Bromich Albion. Seventh in the First Division might be all right for some clubs. For others it would even be seen as success. For Arsenal, it was failure.

But I wasn't looking back when I arrived at Highbury, walked up the stairs and through the marble halls to see manager Don Howe. The subject for discussion was my new contract and I was expecting to hear the sort of deal that would keep me at the club I had loved since I first walked into Highbury as a kid with a head full of dreams 12 years earlier.

Don, who had taken over from Terry Neill as manager when a lot of people thought he might get the sack too, didn't look happy. We both knew why I was there. It didn't need any pleasantries. He came straight to the point. "They are offering you a new one-year deal – with no more money."

I was stunned. Arsenal, the way I saw it, had no more need of me. They were more or less inviting me to find another club. So this was the reward for staying loyal. For thinking that Arsenal would believe in me the way I had in them when first Brady and then Stapleton left to better themselves abroad and at home. It wasn't the money aspect that upset me. It was the feeling that the club I had served so faithfully no longer wanted me.

"Look," said Don. "I'm going away with England to Mexico and the United States. I hope you are here when I come back. I don't want you to go. I swear to you I told the board they should keep you."

My mind, as I drove home to Cockfosters in Hertfordshire, was in turmoil. When I look back now it is something of a minor miracle that I didn't crash the car.

I had harboured hopes that I would get a testimonial in the season that was just ended. Instead, Pat Jennings had got one – a couple of weeks earlier. I didn't begrudge Pat his match. He was, after all, one of the game's all-time greats. He was also my best friend.

Thinking back, it seemed strange that there was a time when Liam Brady, Frank Stapleton and I were known at Highbury as Dublin's 'Big Three'. Liam went, and then there were two. Frank departed, and it was just me. Now, it seemed, I was to be on my way too.

Liam had made it clear early on in his last season that he wanted to take his immense talent abroad. Frank, I think, would have stayed if Arsenal had been prepared to match what he got at Manchester United. They weren't – and he went. A lot of money has since been spent trying to replace him. I stayed, signing for another four years.

Now those four years were up. Coming away from Highbury that Monday morning I couldn't help thinking what Frank had said when I saw him a month after his move to Manchester United. We were on our way to play for the Republic of Ireland in Holland.

"I hope they've made it worth your while to stay," he said.

"I stayed in the hope that the club would reward me with a testimonial," I replied.

David O'Leary (Arsenal)

He shook his head, gave me a funny look and murmured, "You're a mug, son."

Soon after Liam Brady had left for Italy, I genuinely think the chance might have been there for me to follow him to Europe. Liam had remarked several months after signing for Juventus, "You're as good as any centre-half over there. Do you want me to look round for you?" Torino was later mentioned as a possibility. Then there was Bayern Munich. I know they wanted me at the time Frank went to United and my own contract was up.

Now it was the summer of my discontent. Loyalty? I was beginning to wonder whether it had any meaning in football.

The day after meeting so briefly, and so bitterly, with Don, I flew to Scotland to see my brother Pierce play in the Scottish Cup final for Celtic against Dundee. Celtic won, and as I joined in the celebrations that night, I felt happy for Pierce but rather sorry for myself. I returned to London, then flew to Cork on the Friday to join up with the Republic of Ireland team who were playing Spain on the Sunday. We drew 0-0.

Who should be sitting in the hotel when I arrived in Cork? Frank Stapleton, with his FA Cup winner's medal after Manchester United's Wembley win over Everton, happy as I have ever seen him, and asking, "Everything all right with you?" There wasn't a lot I could say.

Loyalty? I had played most of that season with my nose broken in three places after an incident in a Milk Cup tie at Bristol Rovers on 9 October. But I kept quiet about it and played on . . . week after week, often in pain and often having difficulty with my breathing.

Two weeks after the meeting with Don that had left me feeling let down and utterly dejected I went into the London Clinic for my nose to be put right. As always with Arsenal, it was the best medical attention that money could buy. I have always maintained that no club in the country pays more attention to the welfare of their players. But for five days I could have been dead in there. I didn't get a visit or even a phone call from the club. I was in no mood to lie in a hospital bed. It just made me feel more and more miserable.

As soon as I came out, my wife Joy and I took off to Ireland for a holiday. I left London full of despair. I didn't want to leave Arsenal, and I felt the club knew it. But even with the possibility that I might get a testimonial if I signed again, they were making it very hard for me to stay.

All the time we were in Ireland, Joy could see my mind was over the sea and far away. She said, "Leave Arsenal – and tell the world why." We stayed away for three weeks. There was no word at all from the club – they knew where I could be reached – and I could have gone and signed for anyone.

Loyalty? I had never given Arsenal a minute's trouble. I had always got on with my job, never ever been suspended. I came back for pre-season training in July and found I was an outcast.

John Cartwright, the former England youth manager, had arrived as first-team coach, with Terry Burton reverting to his old job of looking after the reserves and Tommy Coleman leaving the club.

All Don had to say was that I was still being offered a one-year contract on the same terms. Because I wouldn't sign, he didn't play me in any of the early pre-season games and I felt really out of it. It just didn't make sense. I trained with the first team, and every day John Cartwright asked me the same question, "Have you signed?"

Our first friendly was a gentle stroll in the summer sun at Windsor and Eton. I wasn't picked. I went to the game and nobody spoke to me. That was on the Tuesday.

On the Friday, we played at Brighton. Again, the only words I heard from Don were . . . "You're not playing." Tony Adams took my place. In ten years, other than through injury, I had never before missed a first-team match.

Then we had a Sunday game against Tottenham. It was a testimonial at White Hart Lane for their gifted midfield player Glenn Hoddle. I don't to this day know how or why it happened. But suddenly I was part of the picture again. I played.

That evening I had a long talk with my solicitor Michael Kennedy. He is a friend as well as a life-long Arsenal supporter. He said to me, "Look, this is doing nobody any good. It's bad for you, it's bad for the club, and the supporters are wondering what the heck is going on."

That conversation reminded me of how fantastic the Arsenal crowd had always been. Four years earlier, when Frank went to United and my own future at the club was in the balance, I got dozens of letters pleading, "Please don't leave." When I signed for a further four years I got just as many saying, "Thanks for staying." This time, the letters again flooded in asking me not to go. I felt then, and say now . . . it was an important factor in the decision I had to make. The following day I signed – for one year and for the same money. As Michael, my solicitor, said, "You've got to hope that the club will remember you put them first."

At Easter of that 1985-86 season, Don went. It was very sad. I liked and respected him enormously. I still do. When it came to being manager of Arsenal, I always felt he was the right man at the wrong time. Don left after saying in his programme notes that he thought I'd had a good season. I appreciated that.

There was talk of Terry Venables, rumours about Graham Taylor. When another season that had promised so much and produced only disappointment finally came to an end, I turned on the radio to hear that George Graham was the new manager of Arsenal.

I knew that his most successful days as a player had been spent at Highbury. He was remembered as a talented and vital member of the side that did the double in the early 1970s. He had learned his trade at Millwall after working for Terry Venables at Crystal Palace then Queen's Park Rangers. But I knew that Arsenal had always been his only real love. I also knew that I was about to face another contract battle.

George saw me in the same office where I had talked with Don 12 months earlier. I found myself thinking, "I've heard this somewhere before", as he said, "I'm offering you another year – on the same money."

I said, "I'm not signing."

He responded, "Go away and think about it" – adding,

"I'm assessing everybody. And let's face it. Nobody has been doing it around here. You've all got a lot to prove."

All I could think of was that for 13 years I had given the club good and loyal service. During my time, Pat Rice, Sammy Nelson, George Armstrong and Pat Jennings had all been given good testimonials. Why not me?

Three weeks later, George came up to the house. His honesty, his enthusiasm, the things he wanted for Arsenal excited me. I got my testimonial. It was against Celtic, with my younger brother Pierce playing for them, and it was a big success. But I had already decided during that visit by George to commit my future to George Graham and Arsenal.

I'm glad I did. That one-year contract became a four-year deal. It ties me to Arsenal up to my 33rd birthday. I reckon I can still go on for at least another two years after that – at Arsenal if they still want me. I would also like to think I can beat George Armstrong's Arsenal record of 621 first-team games – made up of 500 in the League, 60 FA Cup, 35 League Cup and Milk Cup and 26 European. My total stood at 577 at the end of last season.

Yes, I'm delighted I stayed. I know now that if I had moved on I would have missed the chance of playing for a manager who can become one of the best of all time. That is how highly I rate George Graham.

CHAPTER TWO

In the Beginning

It isn't really surprising that I became an Arsenal player. I was born deep in the heart of Gunners territory at Stoke Newington . . . not much more than a few Pat Jennings drop kicks away from Highbury. My dad was working in England at the time, as a carpenter, and if my grandfather hadn't died a week after I came into the world, forcing the family to return to Dublin, I might be as Cockney now as Kenny Sansom. But back we went to Ireland, where my father Christie now works buying and selling for a freight company that uses the big containers.

My sister Emily, who is three years younger than me, has no interest in football. I can understand and accept why. She grew up in a home where soccer was the main topic. My brother Pierce, who was to play for Celtic, and I rarely talked about anything else.

I was eight years old when England won the World Cup in 1966. I watched the final on television and was absolutely captivated by what I saw. We used to get the football from England on television on a Saturday night. We saw Kevin Keegan and all the big stars of that era. I would sit goggle-eyed pretending, as kids of that age do, that it was me scoring the winner at Anfield, and Arsenal, White Hart Lane and West Ham.

Pierce and I used to go to watch all the teams from England when they came over to the Republic for pre-season warm-up matches. One game I remember vividly – Shamrock Rovers against Everton. I was standing outside afterwards, waiting for the Everton players to get on their bus. This little red-haired fellow came out. I thought at the time he wasn't much bigger than me. But what a player. It was Alan Ball. Before climbing on board, he signed my autograph book. I remember looking at him as he sat on the bus and thinking I would like to be like that one day – a famous footballer, the idol of thousands, waiting to be whisked off to the airport.

How was I to know then that the day would come when we would be sitting together for hours at a time on buses all over the world, sharing the same dressing-room bench and the same hopes and ambitions? I have to say that when I arrived at Highbury as a raw youngster no player gave me more help and advice than Alan.

At school, I was never allowed to play soccer. It was a Christian Brothers school. So hurling and Gaelic football, the traditional Irish games, were the sports on the curriculum. It was daft really because as soon as the last bell of the day went, I was out of school, straight home, and in the fields nearby playing soccer. Most of the boys in my class were with me.

I recall one weekday afternoon going to Lansdowne Road. There were no floodlights and the Republic were playing Russia. I was 12 and a member of the Shelbourne Boys' team at the time. Half the school was there. The following morning, almost everyone seemed to be carrying a note saying sudden illness had prevented attendance the previous day. When it came to my turn to explain my absence, the headmaster said, "Don't bother. I know where you were yesterday afternoon."

The Christian Brothers are missionaries who teach in Africa and throughout the Third World. Discipline in their schools is very strict. The education is of the highest order. Looking back, I have to say it didn't do me any harm. I might have been football-daft but I wasn't too much of a duffer at my lessons. I got the equivalent of seven out of nine 'O' levels, including Maths, English, History, and Gaelic language, which I used to be able to speak fluently. I failed Woodwork, which didn't please my father.

For all that, he made sure I didn't go short of anything when it came to pursuing my dream of making it as a footballer. I never, like a lot of the kids I knew, played in borrowed boots. Adidas boots, when I grew up, were all the rage. But you couldn't get them in Ireland. A shop which sold them in Southampton advertised in one of the football magazines. My uncle sent over. Two months later I was the owner of a pair of boots.

I was 12 years old and already knew quite firmly that centre-half was my position.

A lot of people think Liam Brady, Frank Stapleton and I all arrived at Arsenal around the same time. But I was still at Shelbourne when they were beginning to make their mark at Highbury. Liam is three years older than me, Frank two years older. The only occasion I ever met Frank before we teamed up at Arsenal was when I went to Manchester United for a trial. I was only 13. Frank was a trialist at the same time.

United, around then, had their former Irish right-back, Shay Brennan, at Waterford as player-manager. He recommended me to United. He had seen me playing for the Shelbourne Under-14s. Frank O'Farrell was the Manchester United manager. I was there for two weeks and I remember playing at The Cliff, United's training ground, with players who are still at Old Trafford. Paddy Crerand was in charge of United's youth section and he always says to me whenever I see him, "Why didn't you sign for a good club when you had the chance?"

They must have liked what they saw in those two weeks. At the end of my fortnight they asked me to sign schoolboy forms. But it was the Easter holidays and I was there just to enjoy myself. I had to get back to school.

United's scout in Ireland, Billy Beehan, came up to the house when I returned home. But my dad was very firm. He refused to let me sign the forms that would have given Manchester United first option on my future services. He felt if they still wanted me in a year's time, United would come calling again. They had everything to gain. But where was the benefit for me? There was no law saying thay would have to take me in a year's time.

I always tell schoolboys not to commit themselves to one club. At the age of 13 and 14 there is no need for them to make that sort of decision.

Still, those two weeks I spent with United remain to this day a memorable experience. I stayed with Shay Brennan's mother in Wythenshawe. I used to get the bus in to Old Trafford and go up to The Cliff in the club van. There were usually hundreds of fans waiting outside – with George Best always the number one target for the autograph hunters. I played in practice games with all the stars and was once flattened by first Willie Morgan and then David Sadler. It was a lot for a young boy from Ireland to take in.

It was in those two weeks that I had my first experience of

We're all a bit smarter now – I hope. John Murphy, myself, Frank Stapleton and Liam Brady.

the atmosphere that makes Old Trafford so special on a big match day. Paddy Crerand took all the trialists to watch Manchester United play Derby. The size of the crowd and the excitement that was generated took my breath away.

As I went home to Ireland, Frank Stapleton was going on to Arsenal for trials. He finished up by signing for the Highbury club. It is ironic that nearly a decade later United had to pay £800,000 to get him to Old Trafford – and Arsenal thought then that he was undervalued by the Independent Tribunal.

Just after my visit, Frank O'Farrell left United. Three years later, Frank Stapleton and I met Mr O'Farrell in Iran when we were there with Arsenal's youth team. He was Iran's national coach. He came up to me and Frank, asked how we were getting on and said he remembered us well. He was a lovely man. I've never seen him since.

But before that, it was back to Ireland and school for me. I was playing for Shelbourne Under-15s when I got into the Republic Schoolboys team. All the scouts from England were over and at Easter, when I was just 15, I was invited for trials by Arsenal. I had been recommended by Bill Derby, Arsenal's scout in Ireland.

I spent a week at London Colney, Arsenal's training centre. Bertie Mee was manager of the club at the time, with Gordon Clark the chief scout and Dave Smith the man who looked after the trialists. At the end of the week, Mr Clark said he wanted me to sign for Arsenal as an apprentice professional. He came over to Dublin in May and I signed the forms that made me an Arsenal player. Mr Clark said I would be expected to report for pre-season training in July.

My mum said at the time that she would never forgive dad for letting me leave home at only 15. I think, by now, he might just have been forgiven!

Soon after signing for Arsenal, I played for the Republic Schoolboys at Dalymount Park. Gordon Clark came over for the game. Afterwards, he came back to our house in my dad's car. I reckoned I had played well. I was a bit full of myself. I thought I knew it all.

Mr Clark soon changed that. He looked at me, shook his

head and said, "Son, you've got so much to learn. Are you really the same player I signed at Easter three weeks ago?" I knew then that the road to the top was going to be long and hard.

CHAPTER THREE

Learning to be an Arsenal Player

I arrived at Arsenal on 15 June 1973 to learn the trade of being a professional footballer. As an apprentice, glamorous it wasn't.

It was the Highbury era of Bob Wilson, Alan Ball, John Radford, Eddie Kelly, Jeff Blockley, Peter Simpson, Ray Kennedy and Peter Storey – all of them big names to me and intimidating characters.

I was put into digs in Southgate. The apprentices would be picked up by club bus in the morning and taken to London Colney. Bertie Mee, the manager, was a stickler for punctuality. We would get to Colney at about ten minutes past ten. Training started at 10.15 and there were no excuses for being late. My first job was to pump up the footballs to be used in training that day. I had five minutes for this task and in that time I also had to get changed. I followed this pattern for a full year. After training, the apprentices had to fill the baths for the first-team players. When they were finished, we tipped out the dirty water and cleaned out the tubs.

Tony Donnelly, who was the kit manager then and still is, was like a sergeant major. The other apprentices told me he was from Dublin. I thought, well, he will like me. I'll have no problems. Did I get favoured treatment? Not at all. In fact, I used to think that if I ever made the first team I would make his life a misery the way mine seemed to be in those early months. I wouldn't forget all the things he made me do. It was as I grew older that I realised it was all part of the Arsenal way – aimed at making you a better person as well as a better player.

It didn't take long to find out what being an apprentice means. The day before every first-team match at Highbury we would be at the ground cleaning out the dressing-rooms. The toilets too. This was Arsenal. Everything had to be spotless. In that first year I was on away team dressing-room duty – or jankers as we used to call it. Bertie Mee would come round at three o'clock on a Friday afternoon and check everything. That would include the boot-room. If there was a speck of dust, you heard about it. Nobody moved or left for the day until he was satisfied.

When I came to the club there were 12 apprentices. At Christmas, a lot of them had reached 17 and they signed as full professionals. That left five of us – with double the work load.

In that first year, I only got into the Youth team for the South-East Counties League matches. When it came to the Cup games, the older boys like Liam and Frank, who were by then in the reserves, would return to the Youth side.

I was now, besides pumping up the footballs and doing the dressing-rooms, having to scrape the mud off all the first-team boots before they went to Tony Donnelly for polishing. Behind the dressing-rooms at Highbury is a room with a long wall. At one end would hang the apprentices' boots. In the middle, were those belonging to the young professionals, and at the other end those of the first-team squad. You could gauge how your career was going by where your boots were hanging. If you stayed down the far end too long you were really struggling.

That first year was hard. I was a 15-year-old away from home and the physical training used to leave me exhausted.

I arrived at Arsenal thinking I was already a good player. I soon found I had everything to learn.

Every six weeks, the apprentices who stayed in digs were sent home. We would leave after the Youth game on a Saturday and come back the following Wednesday. It was typical of the considerate way Arsenal look after their players. But it was also unsettling. John Murphy, another Irish player who joined Arsenal at the same time as me, couldn't cope. He went home one weekend and didn't come back. It was homesickness.

After John quit, there were times when I wondered whether I would follow him. There I was, not much more than 15, saying goodbye to my family and making the journey from Dublin to London on my own. I would get to Heathrow Airport and catch a bus to Hounslow West. From there, it would be the underground to Southgate. I didn't have any relatives over here. I used to quietly cry all the way from Dublin. In the end I stopped going home. It was too upsetting.

Bertie Mee, I have to say, was fantastic. On a training day he would spend about half an hour with the first team, go and watch the reserves train and then move over to the youth team who were working with Ian Crawford. Bertie never coached the first team. He was more of an overlord. He knew everything that was going on at the club. He made sure that the youth team players were never strangers to him. I appreciated that. As an organiser, Bertie was in a class of his own.

I can't say I took to Ian Crawford. He was a bit too hard, too cutting in what he had to say. I always felt he thought he was dealing with experienced senior players – not kids learning the game. Nobody in that youth team of my first year is with Arsenal now.

The wages for an apprentice didn't exactly allow you to live a life of luxury. I was on £5 a week plus an underground pass from Cockfosters to Arsenal, nine stops down on the Piccadilly Line. I didn't need much more.

At that age and at that stage of my career I wasn't there to live it up in the West End of London. Most nights I would just go back to the digs and watch television. I didn't drink anything stronger than orange juice or Coke. But I have seen plenty of apprentices, no older than 15, downing a pint. I'm not criticising them. That was their way. But it wasn't mine.

Graham Rix, with whom I later shared so many good times at Arsenal is about my age and didn't do his time as an apprentice. He signed straight off as a professional and missed out on the non-football chores such as cleaning out the dressing-rooms.

The youth team games were nearly always played on Saturday mornings in the London area. Later we would all come back to Highbury and be given 25 pence to go to the fish and chip shop up the road . . . then get back for the first-team or reserve game in the afternoon.

My Saturday afternoon job was to clean the away team dressing-room after the match. That chore extended, of course, to night matches. I was seeing all my heroes of a few months earlier face to face.

I used to get all the autographs. This was the era when Leeds United, under Don Revie, ruled and I vividly recall them coming to Highbury on a Tuesday evening and giving Arsenal

Jugglers three. Tony Woodcock and Stewart Robson get in on the act.

a thrashing. I was really busy with my 'book' that night – getting Johnny Giles, Billy Bremner and Allan Clarke, who was never the most happy-go-lucky fellow I ever met in the game. Johnny Giles said "Hello" and I cannot to this day remember whether or not I blushed. How was I to know then that the time would come when I would play in the same international side as one of the greatest footballers ever to come out of Ireland?

Yet the established player who made the greatest impression on me in those early days was Johan Cruyff. He came to Arsenal from Barcelona to play in George Armstrong's testimonial. The apprentices who looked after the home dressing-room were all trying to switch to the away side so they could meet the Barcelona stars. Cruyff went out of his way to talk to me, asking how I was enjoying myself at "this great club" and "what are the duties you have to perform as an apprentice professional?" He was kindness itself. When you are an impressionable kid, you don't forget that sort of thing.

Then there was Leicester City. I always remember them as dandies of those times – the best-smelling, best-dressed team of the lot. The exotic smells that used to come out of their dressing-room were something else. Alan Birchenall always had his hair-dryer with him, while Keith Weller could have stepped out of a tailor's window. They used to take an age to get into their street clothes after a game. Birchenall, Weller and Frank Worthington would stand and examine themselves in the mirror for what seemed hours. And Chelsea, the Chelsea of Peter Osgood and Alan Hudson, were no different. All of this wasn't much good to a youngster who had an underground train to catch to connect with a bus to his digs.

Frank Worthington was the friendliest of characters, though. He would always have time for a chat. The same went for John Hollins when he was a Chelsea player. The Liverpool players were always friendly too. So were the Liverpool staff – Bob Paisley, Ronnie Moran, and the late Bill Shankly. Leeds, I found a close-knit lot. They kept themselves to themselves and said little to outsiders. Tottenham, the Spurs of Pat

Jennings, Martin Chivers, Alan Gilzean, Mike England, Cyril Knowles and Steve Perryman didn't hang about. They came, played the game, and were away within minutes of the final whistle.

I know there were those at Arsenal who had doubts about whether I would make it. But I stayed in the youth team for only the one season. The following year I got into the reserves for the first game against Southampton and kept my place for the whole year. I was 16 and playing alongside Frank Stapleton, Charlie George, Jeff Blockley and Eddie Kelly.

In February of my second season Arsenal played a testimonial match at Reading. I was taken along as substitute. It was my first experience of being with the first team. Chairman Denis Hill-Wood came into the dressing-room before the game and I was introduced to him as a young lad for the future. He said, "I hope you are." It was my first meeting with a man whose death was such a loss to Arsenal and football. I came on in the second half, partnering Peter Simpson in the middle of the defence. Gordon Clark was at the game. He said he was delighted with the way I had played. That pleased me as much as anything.

The other players all had a drink on the coach coming back. I wasn't allowed to. I was still only 16 and an apprentice. That meant going back to cleaning the dressing-rooms and a place in the reserves.

In that second year my money went up to £6 and I was the only apprentice in the second team. Boredom was the biggest enemy. John Murphy, before he went home one weekend never to return, was my biggest pal then. We used to go for walks in the evening and sit in the local Wimpy bar with a hamburger and a milk shake just to pass the time. To this day, I go past that Wimpy bar and remember the days John and I sat there together.

It's funny the way things work out. John went home to take his place in the family business and took up rugby. He was later capped by Ireland as a full-back. I used to watch him on *Rugby Special*.

I never ever complained, lonely as I often felt in those early days. I had great digs. I stayed with Jack and Pam Lewis in Southgate for six years. They treated me like their own son. I would get home from a night match at 11.30 after cleaning the dressing-rooms and Mrs Lewis would always have tea and sandwiches waiting. It was a kindness I never forgot.

I signed professional the following May – on my 17th birthday. It was 1975 and my wages went up to £40 a week but I now had to pay £20 a week for my digs and my underground pass was taken away. That first contract was for two years.

Certain privileges came with being upgraded to full professional. For instance, I was now allowed to wear tracksuit trousers. At Arsenal, apprentices could wear tops, but not bottoms. That still applies. I still used the away team dressing-room. The difference now was that I didn't have to clean it out as well. The home dressing-room was for first-team players only. It still is. Being a full professional also meant I was able to have a better type of boot. I went home to Dublin that summer a happy young man – even though Bertie Mee and Gordon Clark both made it clear I still had a long way to go.

I was six feet, one inch and weighed in at ten stones when I joined Arsenal. At the end of my second season I went home stronger and fitter and weighing over 12 stones.

CHAPTER FOUR

The Irish Connection

There was a feeling on the fringes of Highbury, and it was possibly generated by jealousy, that Liam Brady, Frank Stapleton and I were a bit of an Irish Mafia. But the truth is that the three of us were never that close. We certainly didn't mix together socially. Graham Rix was always Liam's great mate while Frank was something of a loner. In fact, both Liam and Frank were already established at Arsenal when I arrived at the club, and I have to say that nobody could have given me more help or encouragement than Liam.

In the summer of 1975, when I was just 17, Bertie Mee took the first-team squad to Scotland as part of the pre-season build-up. Peter Simpson was injured and I found myself on the trip. I was very nervous. Here I was, two years out of Ireland, still with 'L' plates on and sitting on the coach with Alan Ball, John Radford, Peter Storey, Pat Rice, Sammy Nelson, Jimmy Rimmer and Brian Kidd on a ten-hour journey north of the border. I could see them looking at me and thinking, "Who's this kid? He doesn't say much." I was so overawed at being in such illustrious company I think I blushed when I was asked if I wanted sugar in my tea.

Terry Mancini – or 'Henry' as he was inevitably called – was my room-mate in Scotland. Bertie Mee had bought him for £20,000 from Queen's Park Rangers and I found out much later that the reason behind the signing was that his experience would help develop me as a player.

'Henry' knew he wasn't the best player in the world. But as a character he was in a league of his own. He was one of many who became an honorary Irishman – meaning he could play for the Republic because a mother, father or grandparent was born there. He was prematurely bald and when he went out to play in his first international for Ireland at Dalymount Park he wore a wig – taking it off and waving it to the crowd. When they played the national anthems before the start 'Henry' had to ask, "Which one is ours?"

To 'Henry' every day was a holiday. He always had a smile on his face and I would be surprised if he had an enemy in the world. He was a real smoothie. He drove a Mercedes sports car, wore the latest, most fashionable gear and went to the best restaurants.

We played Hearts, Dundee and Aberdeen on that pre-season tour of '75. I played against Hearts . . . With 'Henry' telling me when we arrived in Scotland, "Don't worry about anything. If you get on, I'll take the knocks."

It was during the warm-up of the Hearts game that Liam whispered to me, "You're good enough son. You can go all the way, you're not just here to make up the numbers."

Liam was, and still is, a great player. He has never claimed to be the quickest. But he has that all-important acceleration over two yards. Going forward, he is superb, with a marvellously accurate left foot.

I was very disappointed when he left Arsenal. I felt we had lost a player it would be impossible to replace. At that time, there wasn't a better midfield man in British football. Yet I knew he was doing the right thing. A lot of people at Highbury, players among them, said he wouldn't be able to cope with the man-to-man marking in Italy. I think the success he had in those first two seasons at Juventus, when they were twice champions, destroyed that theory.

Liam was always more outgoing than me, with a depth of

knowledge about topics other than football that possibly surprised those who didn't know him. Deep down, I think I realised, sad as I was to see him go, that the time was right for Liam to take on a new challenge. He was socialising a lot in those last months at Arsenal. Italy really did mature him.

Certainly, I don't think I ever had an argument, or any sort of disagreement, with Liam. For all that, we didn't have a lot in common. We are different types.

In my early days, I was most at ease with John Devine, another of the Irish contingent at Highbury. Frank Stapleton was someone I found it very hard to get close to. He was a deep thinker – a bit like Johnny Giles. He was also the best, most dedicated trainer I have ever come across. I don't know anyone who worked harder at his game.

When Terry Neill became manager in 1976, I know he was on the point of releasing Frank, who had received a big offer to go and play in South Africa and was considering it.

Special for Daily Mirror *London from Monte Fresco Turin. O'Leary gets between Terry Neill and Don Howe watched by Liam Brady (left) and Pat Jennings.*

Malcolm Macdonald had been signed, he and John Radford were the strike force in pre-season games and Frank was right out of the picture. When we started that season at home to Bristol City, Raddy and Malcolm were the pairing up front and there really didn't seem much future for Frank as an Arsenal player.

The doubters said his control was poor, his first touch awful. Yet four months later Raddy was on his way to West Ham and Frank was in. He had proved a lot of people wrong. The improvement, from working at his game, was incredible.

Frank was just about the most unselfish striker I've played with or against. You could play a ball up from the back confident he would hold it up or lay it off. He was a big lad who was excellent in the air. He was never dirty and I don't ever recall him losing his temper.

Frank left at the end of the season Aston Villa won the League and we finished third. None of us at Highbury knew until we read it in the papers or heard on the radio that he had gone to Manchester United. Frank kept himself to himself. He never told me or anyone else anything. In that respect he was always something of a mystery man.

Ron Atkinson signed Frank for United and he had five good years at Old Trafford. But I always felt his best days were spent with Arsenal. I have also never altered my view that Arsenal, as big and as famous as any club in the country, should have been able to keep him. We had no one coming through in the reserves and Terry Neill and Don Howe didn't want him to go. I don't know what contract Frank got from United. I do know Arsenal were not prepared to match it.

What his departure cost Arsenal is capsuled in the money they have spent trying to replace him. Lee Chapman cost £500,000 from Stoke and was sold for £100,000. John Hawley came for £80,000 and was given a 'free'. Then Ray Hankin had a short spell at Highbury while big money went on Tony Woodcock and Charlie Nicholas. They have gone too.

It's funny the way Liam, Frank and I were bracketed as a trio. I don't think I ever remember the three of us going out

together. Gordon Clark found us all. He was largely responsible for the Irish connection at Highbury.

John Devine, as easy-going and happy-go-lucky a footballer as you could possibly meet, was part of that connection.
John had come over with me in 1973 when we both had a one-
week trial. He eventually joined Arsenal a year later.

A right-back of genuine quality, his ability has never been
questioned. He was particularly good going forward. John
got Pat Rice out of the side, and he kept him out. So much
so that Pat was sold to Watford. But in many ways Rice going,
thus easing the competition for the number two shirt, was
John's undoing. He relaxed. His application became sloppy.
He lost his way, his place – and finished up being transferred
to Norwich City. I don't think he liked the pressures asso-
ciated with playing for a top club like Arsenal. He was known
as 'Joker' Devine and in those early days we were very close.

*A shoulder to lean on. Pat Jennings was my best pal and he never ever let
me down.*

His deep-down ambition was to be a pop singer. I always roomed with John on international trips with the Republic. He would always take his guitar. It would be all wrapped up and he would tell anyone who asked that it was his golf clubs. Once, we were in Hong Kong with Arsenal – sitting around in the evening, having a drink and just relaxing. A fight started, one that big Willie Young finished. John was up on the stage in the club where we were, doing his impromptu cabaret bit, totally oblivious to the punch-up involving the rest of us.

John liked a drink. He always claimed he got blamed for everything, whether or not he was at fault. John Hollins always used to sit with 'Joker' and me whatever the method of transport . . . train, plane or bus. On that flight to Hong Kong the three of us were together. It was the end of the season, everyone was relaxed and by the time we were a few hours out it is fair to say most of us had downed a fair quantity of red wine. Holly decided the easiest way to dispose of his glass was to throw it back over his shoulder. Whether or not he knew there was still some wine in the glass I will never know. It went all over one of the directors.

'Joker' was fast asleep as this particular director rushed down the aisle, shook him awake and said, "I know it was you. Don't you ever do that again." 'Joker' didn't have a clue what he was talking about.

We also, of course, had a formidable Northern Irish contingent at Arsenal. Pat Rice, Sammy Nelson and later Pat Jennings were terrific people. And, of course, manager Terry Neill was from the Six Counties. I think we all proved that Catholics and Protestants can live together in genuine harmony. Sammy, for instance, is a Unionist and proud of it. But he would never force his views on you. If you were a friend of Sammy's that was all that mattered. His best friend was Pat Rice, who was a Catholic. They were inseparable.

While I was close to John Devine, my best friend among the Irishmen who made Highbury their home over the years was Pat Jennings. He is quiet, he is modest and what you see is the genuine article. He has two loves – his golf and his family.

We lived near each other and would go in together for training in the morning. He would sit beside me in the car and more often than not I would never be able to drag a word out of him. He was the most laid-back person I have ever known.

You could never rush Pat. He wore a watch but we all believed he never looked at it. Time meant nothing to him. Away from football Eleanor, his wife, did nearly everything for him. When we were playing away and had to be down at 11a.m. for a pre-match meal, he would nearly always be late. Don would fret, but Terry would calm him down by saying, "Look, Don, he can't get Eleanor to put his socks on for him. She isn't here."

But Pat Jennings was more than just a tremendous man. He was also the best goalkeeper I have ever known. Even during a game, he never talked. You just assumed he was there – and he always was. Pat took great pride in being a professional footballer and being recognised as the best at what he did.

Pat, like myself, is one of those who hope one day that we will see in soccer – as there is in rugby – an all-Ireland side. I think a majority of the players would favour the idea. But the two Leagues, as well as the rival Associations, would have to come together. And with places in the European tournaments at stake, never mind the World Cup, I can't envisage it happening.

Then there are the officials – on both sides of the border. They value their trips abroad too much. I've been away with the Republic when there have been more officials than players. Very few of these people, and I am sure it is the same with all countries, have the respect of the players.

I remember once, we were going to Bulgaria. You were only supposed to take in one bottle of spirits each. Our plane was loaded down with the stuff. When we touched down at Munich to refuel, the players passed all the duty-free liquor down the aisle and handed it to the driver of the refuelling truck – telling him to keep it. When we were airborne again and it was discovered what had happened, the officials wanted to turn back. Green channel – nothing to declare? Our officials don't know the meaning. If they passed through that way, it would be only in error. As a mark of how much respect the players felt for the officials, Ray Treacy, Don Givens and Terry Conroy used to take great delight in pinching the passports of the committee men and putting them in post-boxes!

If the two Irelands were to unite during my playing years, I wouldn't have to think too long and too hard about a choice for manager. It would be Johnny Giles. He would have the respect of everyone – North and South, Protestants and Catholics. John wouldn't care what you were, as long as you could play the game.

With brother Pierce before my testimonial against Celtic at Highbury.

CHAPTER FIVE

The Family

We are a close family, the O'Learys. My mother, Margaret, and my father, Christie, wouldn't have it any other way. I am the eldest of three children. Sister Emily is three years younger and brother Pierce two years my junior.

Pierce isn't just my brother. He is also my closest friend. Like me, he is a professional footballer. While my first taste of the paid game was at Manchester United as a 15-year-old, Pierce was 16 when he crossed the water for trials with Coventry City. Gordon Milne was manager there at the time, with Terry Yorath among the better known names at the club. They wanted him to sign, but Pierce didn't want to leave home. Johnny Giles was back in Ireland then, in charge at Shamrock Rovers, and Pierce went there instead.

Since then, he has won League Championship and Cup medals with Celtic. But he certainly went round the world on his way to collecting them. Pierce was in his first year in Shamrock's first team – like me he is a central defender – when Gordon Clark, the same Gordon Clark who signed me for Arsenal, came with one of the owners of Philadelphia Fury to see him play.

It was the time, in 1978, when vast fortunes were being spent in a bid to establish soccer as a major spectator sport in the United States through the North American League. Pierce was 18 when he was invited to spend a summer season at Philadelphia. Johnny Giles was a player for the summer with Fury too. Alan Ball was manager.

In 1981 Pierce joined Vancouver Whitecaps, where Giles was then the manager. Vancouver is a beautiful city. Joy and I went for three successive summers to see Pierce and fell in love with the place. I know that in Pierce's first season in Vancouver, Bob McNab, who was on the staff there and had played with me at Arsenal, recommended him to the Highbury hierarchy. Again, Pierce said "No". Pierce married a Canadian girl, Kerry, while he was with Vancouver and was the last player to leave the Whitecaps in November 1984, after the collapse of the North American League. David Hay then signed him for Celtic.

Pierce and I have played together three times in the Republic team. We won twice and lost once. There was a 1-0 World Cup victory over Holland in Dublin, a 1-0 defeat against Northern Ireland in Belfast when we lost to a Gerry Armstrong goal, and a 1-0 win over Belgium.

At club level, I always try to see his big games if Arsenal are not playing the same day and Pierce always makes the effort in reverse. In fact, he is my lucky charm. He was at Wembley when Arsenal beat Manchester United in the FA Cup and again when we won against Liverpool to collect the Littlewoods Cup. It works the other way too. I was there, after all, when Celtic beat Dundee in the Scottish Cup. Pierce, by the way, also has an Irish Cup winner's medal that he collected with Shamrock.

We are not that similar as players. I'm more right-footed than left. Pierce is all left side – left-footed as well as left-handed. He couldn't trap a bag full of cement with his right foot. I think, and Pierce would probably agree, that I'm a bit quicker than he is. I used to win a lot of things in school running events and I once finished third out of 150 in the Leinster Schools' cross-country. It probably explains why I never minded Don Howe's gruelling cross-country runs. Running isn't Pierce's strong point.

Where I like to dress casually, you will rarely see Pierce without a collar, tie and jacket. He also loves cars, particularly fast cars. Me – I'll drive anything on four wheels as long as it gets me where I want to go.

Pierce also needs his sleep. He's usually in bed by 9p.m. I am more of a midnight man, usually watching a bit of television before I turn in.

I have never had any business interests, always being a one hundred percent football man. I have never had an agent. I've never seen the need. Pierce is in business with Celtic goalkeeper Paddy Bonner. They have an industrial cleaning firm, with a contract to clean Glasgow buses.

It's funny the way things work out. As a kid, Pierce was a Celtic fanatic whereas I supported Manchester United because of George Best. I thought he was the greatest.

I'm 21. With my mum and Pierce at a party to celebrate the big day back home in Dublin.

Pierce and I talk on the telephone every week – usually after the games on Saturday. We like to compare notes on how things went and to exchange gossip. I will tell him what is going on down here. He will give me the lowdown on what is happening up there.

I know my mother and father are proud of us both. But mum never comes to a game – unless it is an international and it is being played in Dublin. She doesn't like the big crowds. She came over for the Littlewoods Cup final when we beat Liverpool. But she preferred to baby-sit and watch the match on television while my wife Joy came to Wembley. I don't think she saw too much of the game. Our son John, who was four then, kept saying, "Silly daddy. Why can't I watch the cartoons?"

My father likes to try to get over to see the big games. But he is careful that, if he sees me play one time, he will go and watch Pierce on the next occasion. Deep down, I think mum is a bit of a Liverpool fan. She always liked Kevin Keegan.

Dad is very keen on his football. I think, though, he would concede that my uncle Paddy leaves him well behind when it comes to fanaticism. Paddy is a football nut. He still buys every football magazine published and all the Sunday newspapers to read the match reports. He tapes every game on television and will go anywhere to see Pierce and me play. His idols were always Bobby Moore and Franz Beckenbauer. He loves to see me get forward with the ball and use it the way they did. I have to send every programme of every game in which I play over to Ireland for him.

It hurt my family very deeply when Jack Charlton wouldn't pick me for the Republic team.

I was 23 when I got married. I first met Joy when I was 19 and she was 17. She was working in a travel agent's office at Hertford at the time of our wedding. Her family lived very close to Wilf Dixon when he was assistant manager at Arsenal. She used to enjoy horse-riding and had hurt her knee in a fall. Wilf brought her to Highbury to see Fred Street, who was then the club's physiotherapist. She was waiting for a lift home when we met and started talking.

Later, when we began seeing each other regularly, her father checked me out. I could understand that. He is a Tottenham season ticket-holder and a regular at Spurs games.

Joy was a big hit with my parents from the first time they met. My mother threatened never to allow me back into the house if I didn't marry her. I'm delighted to say I did but I have to admit to being useless around the house. The other players at Arsenal all say I go home, and if anything is wrong, I let Joy get on with it.

CHAPTER SIX

Neill – A Traumatic First Year

It was March 1976 . . . and the last part of a season in which I was to play 32 League games as a 17-year-old. For me, things had gone well. For the club, one disaster seemed to follow another. Alan Ball had fallen out with Bertie Mee, wasn't in the side early on, and Eddie Kelly became captain.

I made my debut in a goalless draw at Burnley and at Christmas Bertie called me in, said I had done well and deserved a rise. I got one – it was £6 ! It put me on £46 a week, which wasn't exactly generous. Still, I didn't mind. I was happy just to be in the side.

On 9 September we had gone to Everton in the League Cup and drawn 2-2 in the first round. In the replay at Highbury we lost 1-0. There was little doubt in everyone's mind that the team was on the blink. On 3 January we went to Molineux and were crushed 3-0 in the third round of the FA Cup by a very good Wolves side.

March came, West Ham were thrashed 6-1 at Highbury and there was a feeling that things might at last be looking up as we left for a short break at Bournemouth. Bertie, as he always did when Arsenal were in that part of the world, went to the chairman's Hampshire home for lunch. He came back later

Terry Neill and I testing out "Super Turf" at Arsenal's new training centre.

that afternoon to tell us, "I won't be with you next year. I'm finishing at the end of the season." We were all stunned. I was particularly shocked. Bertie was manager when I signed for Arsenal and my parents had only allowed me to leave Ireland because they respected and trusted him totally.

Bertie wasn't the greatest on the game. He wasn't a coach. But he was a great organiser. He got the right people around him and he knew how to get the best out of players. He wanted you to realise that being an Arsenal player meant you carried a special responsibility. He was very strong on discipline. When we walked into a hotel – and they were only the very best hotels with Bertie – there was hell to pay if your tie wasn't knotted and the top button of your shirt done up. Bertie was a bit of a nagger and he was inclined to be over-fussy, but I liked him enormously. He wanted the best but he was always there to help when you were in need of advice.

When he made his shock announcement to the players, there were still nine games to go. We finally finished a disastrous 17th in a season when Liverpool won the First Division, pipping Dave Sexton's exciting Queen's Park Rangers side by a single point.

The question, from the moment Bertie said his time was up, centred on who would take over. Bally and 'Henry' Mancini called a players' meeting and asked if we would back coach Bobby Campbell. Bally said that if we said "Yes" he would go to the board and tell them Campbell was the man the players wanted.

I think Ball and 'Henry' were being a bit selfish – taking the line that if they helped Campbell get the job he might find spots for them on the coaching side. The older players seemed to like the idea of Campbell as boss. The younger ones didn't want to get involved. I had no complaints about Bobby. He had helped me a lot – but privately I felt it was time for a change. The club needed new ideas, fresh leadership.

Summer came and I was at home in Ireland when I heard on the radio that Terry Neill had been appointed manager of Arsenal. I had no strong feelings one way or the other about his getting the job. When he was in charge at

Tottenham he had always been very friendly whenever I met him.

The end of season break, I was discovering, went all too quickly. Yet this time, I was eager to get back. I felt that eventful times were ahead of us all. How right that turned out to be.

On his first day in charge at Arsenal, Terry Neill called all the players together in the dressing-room. His message was blunt and simple: "This club needs a good shake-up. Anyone who doesn't agree . . . there's the door. Now let's get down to work."

There were players at Highbury, such as Pat Rice, Sammy Nelson, Peter Storey, John Radford, George Armstrong and Peter Simpson who had played in the same Arsenal side as Terry. It must have been a strange situation for them and certainly a difficult one for Terry. Nor was it a happy, united outfit that Terry inherited. Jimmy Rimmer, whose outstanding form in goal had saved us from relegation the previous season, was arguing about a new contract. He had never been the most popular player at Highbury, but nobody ever questioned his dedication or his ability.

I was called into the office by Terry and offered a new contract that put me on £100 a week. I was very pleased. We shook hands on it and he said, "You are one of the players who will be the backbone of the new Arsenal."

Terry had brought Wilf Dixon with him from Tottenham as his head coach and assistant manager. That was one of his first mistakes. Wilf just wasn't rated as a coach. In fact, he was looked on as a bit of a disaster.

We had a week together at London Colney before going to a training camp just outside Frankfurt for ten days. Malcolm Macdonald had been signed from Newcastle and came on the trip as the club's bright, new star. It was a pre-season that started badly and got worse. Jimmy Rimmer was still rowing with Terry over his contract and the older players seemed to have made up their minds that Terry didn't know what he was talking about.

Just outside the sports complex in West Germany, where we were based, was a cafe where you could go for a couple of beers in the evening. Often enough those couple of beers quickly developed into quite a few. The senior players started complaining about the training. Eddie Kelly openly voiced his disapproval to the boss of the way things were going and was sent home.

On the first Saturday we went to watch a game locally and came back planning to have a drink in a nearby beer hall. That idea went out of the window when Terry told us we would be training that evening in the gymnasium. Everyone had the hump – with the result that we kicked lumps out of each other. The following afternoon Terry told us we would be training again in the evening. The resentment among the players was close to open rebellion. That was when Alan Ball told Terry it was Peter Storey's birthday and the pair of them were going out to celebrate. Ball and Storey didn't train. The rest of the squad joined them after training and it became a mammoth session. Next thing we knew, Terry had turned up. I thought . . . here we go. But all he did was go up to Bally and say, "Everything OK?" I couldn't believe it. It suggested to me he had lost his grip. Yet the root cause of all the problems, I felt, was Wilf's training. It was dull and predictable.

We had a game with Grasshoppers in Zurich and the following morning flew to Zagreb for a game in Yugoslavia. At breakfast that day, Bally put it to Peter Storey, "Shall we get on a plane back to London?" The mood was bleak. Long coach journeys were involved – and they were horrendous. The shouts were coming from the back of the bus, a dilapidated, smelly old thing with hard seats, "Has Alan Whicker ever been here?"

Terry knew things were getting out of hand. Frankly, I felt sorry for him. He seemed a nice man trying to do his best. But it was a bit like a car hurtling downhill. The brakes have failed and the driver doesn't know what to do. In Ryijeka Terry called a team meeting and said, "We are here because no big European clubs will have us. We have just finished 17th in the league."

The players wouldn't accept that. This, after all, was Arsenal – one of the most famous clubs in the world, the club that, under Bertie Mee, had done the League and Cup double not so long ago. Terry put a ban on drinking in the hotel bar. It was blatantly ignored by some of the players. It was an awful way to set out on a new season.

The start to it came and we lost the opening match 1-0 to promoted Bristol City at Highbury. Frank Stapleton hadn't been picked and there were strong rumours that he would be on his way. Liam Brady didn't play in that one either. He was ill.

Three days later we went to Norwich. Frank came in to partner Malcolm Macdonald. John Radford was left out and Liam replaced Alex Cropley. We won 3-1. The next Saturday we went to Sunderland and drew 2-2. A total disaster had been averted.

But it still wasn't right. The older players remained unhappy with the training and it was obvious we had only papered over the cracks. Mid-way through the season, Terry called us together and asked, "Why is it we lack consistency?"

Bally couldn't resist that invitation. He stood up and said, "The training is a joke. I've had him" – pointing towards Wilf Dixon – "at Blackpool and at Everton. I know what he's all about. I would stay and work all day and night if the training was interesting. It isn't."

I had nothing against Wilf. I just felt he was too old for the coaching job. Less than a month after that, Bally was on his way. Lawrie McMenemy signed him for Southampton.

The season dragged on, with mutterings in the background and the sure knowledge that we would win nothing. Queen's Park Rangers had knocked us out of the League Cup and Middlesbrough hammered us 4-1 in the FA Cup. Both those defeats came in the fifth round. We finished eighth in the League.

During that season, Willie Young was bought from Tottenham, Pat Howard came from Newcastle, and Alan Hudson arrived from Stoke. Huddy rowed with Terry almost from the first day, claiming he had been let down on his contract.

The most consistent player for the second successive season was Jimmy Rimmer. Jimmy, like Frank Stapleton, was a loner. He kept himself to himself. The other players didn't like Jimmy very much. In those days, a pub near Southgate underground station was a favourite after-match watering hole for the Arsenal team. It was reckoned he was there one evening after a game when one of the regulars asked, "How did it go?" "I was OK," Jimmy is said to have replied. "It was the other ten . . . ." The others, when they heard about it, didn't exactly put Jimmy at the top of their popularity parade.

That first year was one battle after another for and with Terry. We were supposed to start training at 10.15. Malcolm Macdonald would often come in at 10.45. Nothing was ever said to him. But then he scored 28 goals that season. What could you say? He wasn't a good trainer. He just wanted to score goals . . . and you couldn't call that a bad habit.

Two of those 28 were among the best I have ever seen. We played Leeds at Highbury and drew 1-1. He turned on the edge of the penalty box and almost broke the back of the net. The ball went into the top corner and I've rarely seen a shot hit with such power. He got a similar goal against Pat Jennings when we drew 2-2 at Tottenham. Willie Young, playing against us, got sent off in that game. Two months later we signed him.

As the season drew to a merciful close it became more and more clear that Terry needed a coach.

On 14 May we went to Manchester United and lost 3-2. I remember, before the game, I was in the corridor outside the dressing-rooms trying to get a couple of extra tickets. Tommy Docherty, then United's manager, came bounding along. All of a sudden, I got this whack on the back, and Tommy, with a big grin was saying, "Do you fancy a move, son?" It was the first time I had ever been tapped!

As soon as the season ended we went to Norway for a few games. Bally had gone and Pat Rice was now captain. It was a trip where one rumour followed another. One of them was that Terry was going to make Malcolm Macdonald captain. We couldn't believe it.

We were in Oslo on the last night, having won all three

matches we played, when Terry outlined what would be happening next pre-season. It shook us all. He said we would be back three weeks earlier than usual because a tour to Singapore and Australia had been agreed. The club were on a big guarantee. Big Willie Young immediately asked, "What are we getting out of it?"

In the hotel bar later, Willie said, "Let's all go up and front Terry in his room." Sixteen of us marched up the stairs and into the manager's room. He had answered the door with just a towel round his waist after taking a shower. We didn't waste words. "What will we get out of this trip?" Willie demanded.

Terry replied, "It will be sorted out when we get back pre-season." But he was visibly shocked . . . adding, "You're under contract, Willie. You'll go where you are told to go."

No play today. It's snow fun really as physiotherapist Fred Street and I accept Highbury just isn't playable.

So ended season 1976-77 – Terry Neill's first as manager of Arsenal.

I had to go away with the Irish international side after that. It meant I had only three weeks off in the summer. In fact, the Wimbledon tennis championships were on when we reported back. Nobody, myself included, was happy. Everywhere you looked, there were long faces. It was obvious the players couldn't take much more of Wilf Dixon. Yet nothing had been done – either about our money or about the coaching situation.

We spent the first week at London Colney. The air was full of bitterness and resentment. Rebellion was again just beneath the surface. There was a general feeling that the club were going to do well out of this tour – and there ought to be some reward for the players. I got the distinct impression that if we didn't get our money, the squad would refuse to make the trip. As the row rumbled on, word came that the chairman had told Terry "we would be looked after". That calmed us down. All that week Terry told us he was trying to get Dave Sexton, who was about to leave Queen's Park Rangers, to rejoin Arsenal as chief coach and was hopeful he would be coming on the trip.

We met up at Southgate on the Friday evening at the start of the trek to Singapore. On the coach to the airport, Malcolm Macdonald realised he had forgotten his passport. That was the first panic. It was rushed to Heathrow for him.

We boarded the flight, settled into our seats, and Terry announced, "There will be no drinking." You could feel the tension mounting.

It was hot and humid in Singapore when we arrived after a long, tiring and alcohol-free flight. But at least we were staying in a hotel with superb facilities. We would train at eight in the morning, finish at ten and have the rest of the day to ourselves. It wasn't so bad. We were sitting around the pool when Terry let it be known, "Dave Sexton is joining us and will be coming out to Singapore in a couple of days." You could see spirits visibly lift at that bit of news. A day or so later, Terry told us, "Sorry . . . Dave Sexton is the new manager of Manchester United."

Wilf Dixon had stayed behind in London and the tour deteriorated into a joke. We played Red Star Belgrade and lost in extra-time. The Yugoslav Vladimir Petrovic played superbly in that match and he was later to join Arsenal. Alan Hudson decided to make a night of it after the game. The late Jock Stein was there in Singapore with Celtic, who were playing in the same tournament. He gave Huddy a tongue-lashing – telling him, "Grow up, son, and behave." It was more clear than ever that Terry was a man who needed help.

The party moved on to Sydney on the overnight flight. We checked into our hotel and went almost immediately to the breakfast room. I was buttering some toast when Malcolm Macdonald marched in and demanded, "Where's Terry Neill? I have never been so humiliated in all my life." We found he had been given a kiddie's fold-up bed in his room.

We played the Australian national side in Sydney – and lost. On the coach coming back Terry said, "Let's all stick together and not panic." I don't know why, but everyone felt a lot better.

Next it was Celtic at Sydney Cricket Ground. We lost that one 2-1. Following the Celtic game, we were leaving the next morning for Adelaide at 8a.m. Everyone was told to be ready and not be late.

We were sitting on the coach, waiting to leave for the airport that morning when Malcolm, Huddy, and George Armstrong piled out of a taxi. Fred Street, then Arsenal's physiotherapist, helped them to get their bags packed and we got to the airport in time for our flight. When we got to Adelaide, Malcolm, Huddy and George again went missing – this time it was between getting off the plane and getting on to the coach for the hotel. Once more, Fred Street had to go looking for them.

Lunch at the hotel brought further confrontation. While we were eating, Terry went over to Huddy and said , "I hope that's tonic water in your glass."

Huddy looked at him defiantly and answered "No, there is gin too."

Following lunch, we all went to our rooms to rest. When

we got down at six o'clock that evening to go training, Terry told us Malcolm and Huddy had been sent home because of their conduct.

The following day we had a meeting about the money. We were due to play Red Star in Adelaide. When Terry was asked by Pat Rice if there had been any developments, he looked puzzled and asked, "What money? You must have misunderstood me."

I remember Sammy Nelson getting up and slamming the door behind him as he walked out. We were all seething as Pat Rice said he was going to see the chairman. Later that day Terry saw us again and said, "You will get something. The chairman guarantees it." Ken Friar confirmed what Terry had told us and things quietened down.

We now had to beat Red Star to go on to the final in Melbourne of what, for Arsenal, had become an unwanted and ill-fated tournament. We played well, but we didn't make it. We did go on to Melbourne but only to fly home the following day.

Denis Hill-Wood, the chairman, was very down. He was liked and respected by all the players and I felt sorry for him. I remember going to see him in the first-class section of the plane. I didn't say directly that Terry needed help, but I felt very strongly that he knew what I was thinking.

It was on the trip that Terry mentioned to me the possibility that I would be offered a ten-year contract. I asked Ken Friar about it. He looked puzzled and said he knew nothing.

We got home and I felt the previous few days had been nothing less than a nightmare. We had six days to rest and recuperate and it was back to London Colney to prepare for the League season. It was there that Terry announced, "Don Howe will be joining us as coach tomorrow."

Pat Rice lifted his eyes to the heavens and said, "Good God. You won't know what hit you with this fellow."

I could tell, though, that he was pleased. It took me only a few days to see what Pat meant. But it was just what we needed. It was to be the start of a new era for one of the game's great clubs.

CHAPTER SEVEN

Forward with Howe

One man wasn't entirely happy about Don Howe's return to Highbury – Denis Hill-Wood. A few days before the start of the new season I was chatting to the late chairman. He made it clear that Don would not have been his first choice as coach because of the way he had left the club after the double triumph.

I had already heard from the players who were with Arsenal at the time that Mr Hill-Wood had been very upset at the way Don resigned to become manager of West Bromich Albion and took two key members of the staff, Brian Whitehouse and physiotherapist George Wright with him. I got the impression though, that the reason Don left was because he didn't get the recognition, financially and otherwise, he felt he deserved for the immense part he played in masterminding the League and Cup double.

But Mr Hill-Wood was a forgiving man. He was also a realist. "The club comes first. It is bigger than any of us," he said. "If the manager believes Don is the man for the job, then it is OK by me. It has always been Arsenal's policy that the manager makes the decisions and the board don't interfere."

Terry told us on the Monday of Don's return. In the 48

hours that followed I was to be made well aware of the demanding standards he would be setting. People like John Radford and Peter Simpson still spoke of him with awe. Peter Storey, who had left the club by then, had always said Arsenal started to go downhill after Don left the first time.

Don appeared at London Colney on the Wednesday. He didn't take the training that day. Terry did. Wilf Dixon was nowhere to be seen. Don just stood on the touchline, not saying anything, not taking any notes. But it was obvious he was not missing a thing. I hadn't seen the players so keen, so committed, for more than a year. The tackles were flying in. Everyone, me included, wanted to impress.

The following day, Don took over the training. By the end of it, I was left in no doubt things were changing. I hadn't trained so hard in all my life – and you have got to remember we had already been at it four weeks because of the tour.

From Day One, everybody was behind Don. He asked Pat Rice, George Armstrong and the other senior players where they thought it had been going wrong. The general opinion seemed to be that the training wasn't good enough or varied enough and that Wilf, nice man that he was, didn't have much idea. Don didn't ask me or any of the younger players for our views.

My early impression was of Don being surprised that the players called Terry Neill by his first name – and not "Boss". It was soon obvious that Don would be the 'baddy' in this partnership and Terry the 'goody'. In fact, it made them an ideal pairing. For the seven-and-a-half years they were to remain together, Don played a key role in the coaching and the tactics. Terry was the administrator . . . the front man . . . the office manager.

Don was still living in Wolverhampton at the time he returned to Arsenal. Yet, whatever the weather, it could be thick snow or traffic-stopping fog, he was never ever late for training.

It was two months past my 19th birthday when Don made his Highbury coaching comeback. I soon found that he was not a man for dishing out praise. The less he said to you, the better. It meant you were playing well and doing your job. He gained my immediate respect. He was very passionate about the game, caring deeply about the image that was presented to the public. I have heard players call him a bully, and in some ways he was. But that was only if he thought your attitude was wrong, that you were not giving a hundred per cent. Don didn't like slackers.

There was also what I always considered a very unfair accusation . . . that Arsenal, because of Don Howe, were a side that concentrated on defence. It was rubbish. Don didn't want to concede goals. Tell me a coach who does? But we got stick because we defended well. To me, that never did make sense. We didn't push up for offsides the way manager George Graham likes us to now. Don wanted us to go out and win games and he didn't ever restrict Alan Hudson or Liam Brady. He wanted them to get forward.

We had one friendly before the start of that first season under the new management team of Terry Neill and Don Howe – at Luton on the Friday prior to the Charity Shield match in which Kenny Dalglish made his debut for Liverpool. If Dalglish was to become an outstanding asset to the Merseyside club, then Arsenal were going to be able to speak with equal awe of the man who made his debut for us at Luton – goalkeeper Pat Jennings.

He crossed North London to join us for what I understand was £50,000 – an absolute giveaway – from Tottenham. Pat replaced Jimmy Rimmer, who had gone to Aston Villa. Jimmy, excellent 'keeper that he was, left behind few friends at Highbury. I think the players at Arsenal felt about him the way I heard the lads at Tottenham felt about Steve Archibald. They respected his ability but didn't put him at the top of the list when it came to sending out invitations to a party.

When Terry Neill signed Pat Jennings, he signed the best goalkeeper in the country – better even than Peter Shilton and Ray Clemence. We just could not understand Tottenham letting him go. He had so much natural ability. He took great pride in his performance. And he had this incredible presence. Over a season he was worth 15 goals to us.

After that game at Luton, I went for a meal with Pat Rice and Pat Jennings. I felt pleased to have been invited along. Pat Jennings wanted to know about Don. Pat Rice left both of us in no doubt, saying, "Don will get it right – you'll see."

The days when it was possible to swing the lead and get away with it were gone. There was a new spirit, a new determination around the club. We were to be tighter and more compact at the back. The midfield were under orders to hustle, to get up and support the forwards and to get back and defend when the other side had the ball. We all knew we had a job to do.

Discipline was tightened up all round. Don made it clear. "We start training at 10.15. That applies to everyone. There will be no exceptions. If you are late, I've got plenty of time in the afternoon to devote to you." Don made sure Malcolm Macdonald got the message he was no different from anybody else. He would start on time in the morning and his game would be about hard work as well as goals.

Over dinner that evening after the Luton game, Pat Jennings asked Pat Rice, "How's big Willie?" He had played with Willie Young at Tottenham.

Pat replied, "Don won't put up with him . . . no way."

In fact, Willie stayed at Highbury another four seasons, became a bit of a cult figure with the fans, and played the best football of his career under Don.

Our first League game of that season was at Ipswich. We lost 1-0. Don pulled off Liam Brady before the end. That had never happened to Liam before and he wasn't too pleased. But it was obvious that reputations counted for nothing with Don.

We played Everton at Highbury the following Tuesday night – and won 1-0 through a Richie Powling goal. Don said, "Well done . . . but there is a lot of hard work ahead before we get it right." I didn't hear anyone argue.

Yet Don, I was to find, could be a bit pig-headed. For instance, he had this obsession about the double team. He told us that in the double days he had a team meeting every month where players could have their say. He reintroduced those

Sharing the shade with my old mate Willie Young before our FA Cup final triumph against Manchester United.

meetings. He would ask for our opinions. He wanted to hear things that matched what he himself was thinking.

He was the same with Terry Neill. I can remember on one occasion, Terry said something. It was as if Don hadn't heard a word Terry was saying. Once, I heard him say to Terry during the interval of a match at Ipswich, "If you don't sort these players out, I'm off." They even heard him in the corridor outside.

Don was not the warmest of men. He kept his distance and didn't encourage players to get too close to him. In those days he didn't want to know about contracts. He would say, "That is for you and the manager to discuss. You must go to him if you have a problem. I'm the coach."

When Terry left Arsenal, Don went on record as saying he had never had anything to do with team selection. I couldn't understand that. I believe he totally influenced Terry's thinking. Terry was the front man all the way down the line. He did the public relations bit – and he did it brilliantly. He seemed to enjoy going back to work in the office in the afternoons, speaking at dinners, dealing with the press, radio and television. And to be fair, while he was manager, he always gave Don full credit for his part in any success we had – publicly and privately. Don could have no complaints on that score. Terry was always fulsome in his praise of Don.

We finished that season fifth in the First Division with 52 points. Nottingham Forest won the League with 64 points. We got to the League Cup semi-finals, losing 2-1 to Liverpool over two legs.

Our closest brush with glory was to come in the FA Cup. We started in the third round on 7 January 1978, by winning 5-0 at Sheffield United. I scored from two yards. Malcolm Macdonald got a couple, so did Frank Stapleton. We had stayed at a luxury hotel on the outskirts of the city before the game. The fire alarm went off during the early hours of Saturday morning. I remember Sammy Nelson coming out of his room wearing just his underpants and clutching his wallet. We all had a laugh about that.

The team that had finished the previous season losing 3-2

at Manchester United was Rimmer, Rice, Nelson, Matthews, O'Leary, Young, Brady, Hudson, Macdonald, Stapleton, Armstong. The team that won at Sheffield was Jennings, Rice, Nelson, Price, O'Leary, Young, Brady, Sunderland, Macdonald, Stapleton, Rix. There were significant changes.

David Price had come in after half-a-dozen games of that first season with Don. He was an unselfish player, whose work-rate was phenomenal. He also had a knack of getting vital goals.

Alan Sunderland had arrived from Wolves in November of that season for £200,000. He had tremendous talent. We used him wide on the right early on. But it was later, when he played up alongside Frank Stapleton that we saw the best of him. He had two good feet, a fine first touch, was excellent in the air and as brave as they come. He should have played 30 times for England, but never won more than a 'B' cap. Players got in the England side around that time who were not in the same

Mariner and Mills say "We shall not pass" as Ipswich beat us in the FA Cup Final.

class as Sundy. He was also very independent minded, a stubborn sort of lad. He loved an argument. I remember he actually came to blows with Kenny Sansom when they ran out of words one evening after a midweek Cup game at Plymouth. Kenny and Alan never got on together. Yet even Kenny would probably admit that Sundy's skill could be breathtaking.

Alan, in his early days at Arsenal, used to travel down from Wolverhampton with Don. Alan said that, for two hours, Don's sole topic of conversation would be football.

Graham Rix had taken over from George Armstrong by then. Graham's work-rate was first-class. Sammy Nelson always said he appreciated the cover he got from Graham in those days.

In the fourth round that season we met Wolves at Highbury. All the pre-match publicity surrounded Sundy – with him saying what he would do to Wolves and Wolves trumpeting they knew how to stop him. Actually, there was a lot of respect on both sides. We advanced through a 2-1 win. it was a tight match and we were lucky. Macdonald and Sunderland, with a disputed penalty, got our goals. The penalty came right near the end, and Wolves centre-half Bob Hazell was very upset afterwards.

The fifth round, on 18 February, gave us a home tie with Walsall. The game came three days after Liverpool had blocked our path to Wembley in the League Cup. But we picked ourselves up and won easily – 4-1. I felt particularly low after the Liverpool setback. I felt my first real chance of getting to Wembley had been snatched from me when it looked there for the taking.

Stapleton, who scored twice, Macdonald and Sunderland got the goals against Walsall. They were beginning to look a most effective strike force.

We couldn't complain about our draw in the quarter-finals – Wrexham away. We stayed in Chester the night before the game. Kit manager Tony Donnelly was on the next table at dinner. He was falling about all over the place. We all thought he had been at the bottle. In fact, on the journey down, he had developed a nagging headache. He went up to Fred Street's room, saw a bottle, and took what he thought were two head-ache tablets. They weren't. By mistake, he took two sleeping tablets.

The following day, after Tony had slept better than any of us, we won 3-2. It was a scrappy game and we were a bit lacking in discipline. But thanks to goals from Sunderland, Macdonald and Willie Young we were in the semis.

We drew Orient. No disrespect to them, but we all accepted we would deserve to have our backsides kicked if we lost this one. The game was at Stamford Bridge. Macdonald scored twice, Graham Rix got another and we walloped them 3-0. Lucky Arsenal? Maybe. One of Macdonald's goals was a shot that hit four players on the way in.

Ipswich beat West Bromich Albion in the other semi-final and we went to Wembley for my first final fancying our chances. From semi-finals day through to the 6 May final, Ipswich were battling against relegation. They had injury worries about Kevin Beattie and Allan Hunter. Colin Viljoen complained about not being in the side, and there seemed to be a moan a day from manager Bobby Robson.

We kept quiet about an ankle injury that Liam Brady couldn't shake off. Alan Sunderland, who had missed the semi final, came back at the expense of Graham Rix, who was relegated to substitute. Graham was understandably unhappy. He thought Sundy was the man who should have been on the bench.

Everything went wrong on the day. Pat Rice, who was also struggling with a bad ankle, got a chasing from Clive Woods. Liam didn't last the 90 minutes. He went off and said later he would never again fool himself or the team over an injury. In future, if he wasn't fit he wouldn't play. Roger Osborne got the only goal of the game and we were beaten finalists.

We had been expected to win. But in many ways we beat ourselves. Brady and Rice were not the only ones who played with injuries. Macdonald was struggling with a dodgy knee. Ipswich had so many injuries, or so we were led to believe, that I fully expected half of them to come out on crutches.

We had an inquest at Highbury the following Monday.

Only Alan Hudson, Pat Jennings and I escaped a tongue-lashing. Don said, "We've got to learn from this. We have got to be more professional in future."

Yet it had still been a great season for Don and Arsenal. One final, one semi-final and fifth in the League. Despite the disappointment of Wembley, I was convinced we were on our way.

We didn't have a close season tour and that was a blessing. I went on holiday with Joy to Corfu and I couldn't help thinking about the way things had changed. Particularly the training. Tuesday, for instance, was what Don called his physical day. If there was no midweek game, we would lunch at London Colney and the afternoon would be devoted to stamina running. It involved different sorts of exercises that were designed to make you think and react quickly. If we pleased Don, we would get the Wednesday off. Nobody even thought about slacking on those stamina Tuesdays.

CHAPTER EIGHT

Final Glory – Then Nothing

One season, more than any other, demonstrated to me why footballers need the stamina of a horse bred to win the Grand National to be successful in this country.

It was 1979-80, our third season under the management of Terry Neill and Don Howe, that left every Arsenal player physically and emotionally drained. It was the season when we threatened to win everything – and finished up with nothing. Even now, I get tired just thinking about it. An incredible 69 competitive first-team games were played by Arsenal that season. The wear and tear to muscles was horrendous.

The season before that, 1978-79, was when we tasted final glory – winning the FA Cup. It was my first pre-season with Howe running the training show. To say it was commando-style preparation is no exaggeration. It is not a criticism either.

We went to Heneff, in West Germany, a training complex three-quarters of an hour outside Cologne. On the journey over, the old sweats such as Pat Rice, who had been taken there before by Don, took a special delight in describing Heneff as "Colditz" – without any escape routes. Pat said that nothing we had experienced before could possibly prepare the uninitiated for what was to come . . . . "Cardiac Hill".

I was to find out what he meant. Heneff seemed to consist of the training centre, with hills everywhere you looked. Even going to breakfast in the morning involved going up and down hundreds of steps. The rest of the day, after that, involved climbing up something, somewhere, and then coming down the other side.

Next to "Cardiac Hill" was a running track. Don would organise it so that eight of us worked on the track while the other eight in the squad toiled up and down the hill. You would go straight from the track to the hill. It was reckoned to be 80 metres from the bottom to the top. Don had us running up and jogging down. One day, big Pat Jennings got to the bottom, fell flat on his face, and was as sick as a dog. It was the hardest week of my life.

We would do a lot of ball work in the afternoons. Even then, you couldn't avoid that much cursed "Cardiac Hill". The football pitches were on the other side of "Cardiac" and you had to go up one side and down the other to get to them.

We would finish at 5p.m. and dinner was at 6.30p.m. The food was fantastic. It was the big treat of the day. We didn't go out. There was nowhere much to go. Yet there was no moaning, no talk of rebellion, no attempt by anyone to "go over the wall". The contrast between this pre-season and the previous year was stark. Everyone accepted we were at Heneff to work.

For all that, the season started on a very average note. We played Leeds at home in our opening match and drew 2-2. It was the late Jock Stein's first game in charge of Leeds and the first time I had seen him since that disastrous tour of the Far East. He joked to me before the kick-off, "Don't play too well this early in the season." We didn't. Liam Brady got both our goals in an uninspiring draw. The following Tuesday we drew 1-1 at Manchester City. Eventually we finished seventh in the First Division.

Our high placing of the previous season had won us a place

in the UEFA Cup. It was my first experience of European football. We started off in September with a tie against Lokomotiv Leipzig of East Germany. We won the home leg 3-0 and followed that with a 4-1 victory over there. The best of the goals was a rocket header by Frank Stapleton – into his own net!

In Leipzig, we had gone to the stadium the night before the game to train under the floodlights. We had to use a lift to get to the pitch from the dressing-rooms. One of the lads queried what would happen if we got stuck in that lift on the evening of the match.

The following day, we got to the stadium and the referee made it known he wanted us and Lokomotiv to come out onto the pitch together ten minutes before the 8 p.m. kick-off. We all crowded into the lift. It started – then stopped. Willie Young had the little lift attendant by the throat, telling him he would find out what the "Highbury swing" was if he didn't get the lift moving – and quick. Funny how we were on our way in no time at all. Willie had that winning way with people!

I roomed with John Devine. Terry Neill had told us after

Winners vs Manchester United 1979.

the game, "We will be leaving at nine o'clock in the morning. Fred Street will give you a knock at eight so there should be time for anyone who wants breakfast." I got up after Fred's knock on the door and went for some coffee. Then we were all on the coach ready to go when someone asked, "Where's John Devine?" He was still fast asleep. One director wanted to leave him behind, remarking, "You never know, they might not send him back." We all reckoned that a day with the 'Joker' and the East Germans would have a whip-round to pay his fare home!

The next round of the UEFA Cup paired us with Hadjuk Split. The first leg was away on a tight, compact ground with a highly partisan crowd. We lost 2-1 but reckoned it was a good result. We won the return at Highbury 1-0 and went through on the away-goals-count-double rule. Willie Young got the goal and was a real hero that night.

We drew another Yugoslav team, Red Star Belgrade, in the next round. We were again away in the first leg, this time minus 'Chippy' Brady who was suspended. It was a bitterly cold day, and in a vast, grey stadium in front of a 100,000 crowd, we lost 1-0. We were not too unhappy.

In the second leg at Highbury, we drew 1-1 and our European adventure was over. Mark Healey, a little blond winger, signed from Peterborough, played instead of the suspended Brady. He got injured in the second half and Terry and Don immediately told John Kosmina, who was to play for Australia in the World Cup, to get warmed up. One moment he was doing stretching exercises and the next, when Fred Street signalled for him to come on, he had gone missing. We later discovered he had gone down the tunnel to the toilet. While we were down to ten men, they scored. There was a lot of moaning and muttering afterwards.

Still, we had the FA Cup to come. After losing at Wembley to Ipswich the previous season there had been the usual brave words about coming back next year – and this time winning it.

The third round produced a marathon tie with Sheffield Wednesday and going on to win at Wembley appeared to be a lifetime away. January was a month of absolutely foul weather. We had been drawn away at Wednesday and because conditions were so bad we travelled to Sheffield on the Friday by train rather than coach. An Alan Sunderland goal gave us a 1-1 draw and a replay. But what I remember most vividly is the Wednesday fans nearly burying Pat Jennings under a barrage of snowballs.

The replay was at Highbury the following Tuesday. They scored early on and the big clock that has been such a land-mark at one end of the ground was ticking away in front of us. I recall one of the Wednesday players saying to me, "Never mind, you got there last year. Perhaps it's our turn this time." At that moment, Pat Jennings lofted one of his huge goal kicks downfield. The ball bounced over their defenders, 'Chippy' Brady raced after it and whacked a shot into the net. The whistle went immediately. First to signal the goal then the end of the 90 minutes. It stayed 1-1 in extra time. Everyone felt we had wriggled our way out from under the executioner's axe.

The second replay was at Leicester six days later. This time, it was 2-2 after extra time, with Brady and Sunderland scoring the Arsenal goals. Two days on it was back to Leicester again for a third replay. This one finished 3-3. Frank Stapleton scored twice . . . Willie Young, who was becoming a bit of a *Roy of the Rovers* character, got the other goal. We were so evenly matched, both sides were beginning to believe this one could go on for ever.

There was a five-day gap before we all took the now familiar road back to Leicester. This was the one that broke the deadlock, Frank Stapleton and Steve Gatting scored and we won 2-0. An incredible LP of a cup-tie – the most drawn-out I have ever played in – was finally over. During the Wednesday saga we had signed Brian Talbot from Ipswich. There was now a feeling throughout the club that we were on our way to Wembley again.

The fourth round gave us a home tie against Notts County. It presented no problems. Talbot replaced the somewhat unlucky Steve Gatting, who had played in all the Wednesday games and we won 2-0. Talbot scored – so did Highbury's

resident master of surprises, Willie Young. In the fifth round
we found ourselves away to the other Nottingham side,
Forest. On a muddy pitch, we soaked up almost non-stop
pressure for 85 minutes. They conceded a free kick, Liam
Brady floated it in, and Frank Stapleton headed us into the
quarter-finals.

The sixth round was away again – this time to Southampton. I hate playing at the Dell. The pitch is small, the crowd
are on top of you, and if you get pushed over the touchline
you can finish three rows up in the stand.

We played the game on a Monday night – 24 hours after
Liam Brady was presented with the Professional Footballers'
Association award as Player of the Year at the annual awards
ceremony at London's Hilton Hotel. I was voted into the
centre-half's spot in the all-star First Division side and Liam
and I went with Terry Neill to the dinner while Don took the
rest of the team down to Southampton on the coach. The three
of us were to follow on later.

When we got to the dinner, our table places had gone. Liam
and I didn't even have anywhere to sit. Jack Charlton was at
the table. He turned round and said, "The melon is very
good." I wasn't amused. Liam was understandably annoyed.
We finally found seats at a table almost in the corridor. When
the award to the Player of the Year was announced, the television cameras scanned the banqueting suite where the dinner
was being held and couldn't even find Liam. In fact, we were
behind where the cameras were situated. Liam had to walk
miles to collect his award. But it was something he thoroughly
deserved. There wasn't a better, more exciting or effective
player in the whole of Britain that year.

Come the Monday night it looked as if our luck had finally
run out. Phil Boyer put Southampton ahead late in the second
half and that seemed to be it. But near the end we got a corner.
Terry Gennoe, the Saints 'keeper flapped at it and David Price
was able to head in at the back post. The replay was easy. I
marked Charlie George, who came back to Southampton's
side after injury, and we won 2-0. Alan Sunderland got both
the Arsenal goals.

Cup Winners vs Manchester United 1979.

In the semi-finals, we drew Wolves – with Villa Park the neutral venue. Bearing in mind the proximity to Wolverhampton, it didn't seem very neutral.

Two weeks before we met, Brady got injured. Liam, however, remembered his Wembley mistake of the previous year, when he played though not fully fit, and Steve Gatting took his place. We won 2-0. Stapleton and Sunderland, who had become a formidable and feared pairing, got the goals and we were at Wembley again.

We made a vow this time not to read the papers in the week before the final or get involved in the inevitable hype. We played it all very low-key. We also changed our hotel – in the hope it would bring a change of luck, moving from the West Lodge Park, in Hertfordshire, on the Friday night to the Grosvenor House in the heart of Mayfair.

On the Monday and Tuesday of Cup final week we trained at Bisham Abbey, and had a Press Day there on the Tuesday. We had Wednesday off, trained at London Colney on the Thursday and Highbury on the Friday. Terry and Don thought it would help to have a varied week. On the Friday, after training, we went to the Grosvenor House for lunch and prepared ourselves mentally for the big day.

It is a final, that one against Manchester United, I am asked about through the years more than any other game. For heart-thumping drama it certainly took some beating. We were two up, through a Frank Stapleton header and a Brian Talbot shot, with seven minutes to go. I suppose we thought it was won. United stormed back to score twice, and we were on the rack.

People still ask me how I felt. The truth is I didn't have time to think. Almost immediately, we went down the other end and got the winner.

The goal remains firmly fixed in my bank of memories. 'Chippy' Brady made a great run down the left and knocked the ball on to Graham Rix. He sent it to the far post and Alan Sunderland flicked it in.

Steve Walford came on for David Price when we were two goals up. To this day I don't know why. He was a centre-back replacing a midfield man and it upset the balance of the side. We won, though, and nobody was called to account for what seemed a strange substitution.

I was as pleased for Terry and Don, as we celebrated that night, as I was for myself. I had one or two differences with them down the years. But I liked them both – and still do.

Summer came, and we all needed the rest it brought – short as it was. The following season – 1979-80 – was to be the busiest of my life. Before it started, John Hollins joined us from Queen's Park Rangers. He was a genuinely funny man and he stayed that way throughout his time at Arsenal. I found the gaunt, strained guy, so irritable and apprehensive in those final days as manàger of Chelsea, totally unrecognisable from the Holly I knew at Arsenal. Now we had three comedians at the club – Hollins as well as Sammy Nelson and John Devine.

Pre-season was again spent at Heneff. This time it was worse because there wasn't even any novelty value. We knew what was coming.

The playing season started with the Charity Shield game against Liverpool. Don said, "Go out and enjoy yourselves." So we did . . . and lost 3-1. He nearly tore down the wall in the dressing-room afterwards, he was so furious. Don never ever used that expression to us again.

It was a season that for excitement and the draining of energy both nervous and physical, was surely unique. I don't think even the double year or any other season in Arsenal's proud history took so much out of the players. I look back on those 69 games that we played and firmly believe it was fatigue that finally beat us.

Our League campaign started promisingly enough, with an easy 4-0 win at promoted Brighton. We were title challengers for a long while, until eventually finishing a respectable fourth. But it was the Cups that really captured the public's interest.

We started off in the Cup Winners' Cup against Fenerbahce of Turkey. Don had coached out there and knew a bit about them. We won the first leg 2-0 at Highbury. It wasn't a great result. But we had prevented them from scoring an away goal and in Europe that is all-important.

A few of the players had seen the film *Midnight Express* just before we left for the second leg. Nobody even wanted to risk taking in a box of chocolates. There was also a midnight curfew in Turkey at the time because of political unrest. But I think it affected the Press boys more than the players! We drew 0-0 and it was good enough.

The next round took us to Magdeburg in East Germany. We flew to Leipzig for the second leg after narrowly winning 2-1 at Highbury and had a 90-minute coach journey on to our hotel from there.

It was Brian McDermott's first foreign trip. He roomed with Sammy Nelson. It was a situation Sammy couldn't resist. Sammy told Brian you had to watch every word you said behind the Iron Curtain – particularly as all the rooms were bugged. There were radios in the rooms and Brian would only talk to Sammy with the sound turned on full blast. When Brian came down to breakfast the following morning and asked if it was safe to speak, we knew right away what Sammy had been up to. The game was that afternoon and we drew 2-2 to go through. It was a good performance against a very useful team after a dodgy result at home.

Next came IFK Gothenburg. The home leg was no trouble. We won 5-1 and it could have been more. The drama was to come. Flying into Gothenburg two weeks later, the pilot of our special charter announced over the intercom that he had a problem with the landing gear. There was a sudden silence. I think quite a few aboard – players, officials and Press – made a few promises to themselves about the misdeeds they wouldn't commit again if we got down okay.

We did – after circling round and round the airport jettisoning fuel. It was a false alarm. A light on the flight deck panel had failed to function properly. When we stepped outside, it was to a numbing cold. Even with the warmest clothes, it struck right through to your bones. But we got a goalless draw – and the forward march continued.

The team we didn't want in the semi-finals was Juventus.

We got them, with the first leg at home, which was not ideal.

Fixture congestion, because of our success on the Cup fronts, was piling in on us. We had to play Southampton on the Saturday and Tottenham on the Easter Monday before we could turn our thoughts to the Juventus match on the following Wednesday. We were hoping the Monday game with Tottenham would be called off. But Spurs refused to help us. We beat them 2-1 after Terry left out six regular first-team players – Jennings, Nelson, Rix, Sunderland, Stapleton and Price. It was a game in which Paul Davis made his debut and Sunderland, who was substitute, came on for Brady and scored. Spurs were sick. We thought it served them right. Juventus were at the match and couldn't believe we had been forced to play a big derby game 48 hours before a European semi-final. We were tired all right. There was a huge crowd at Highbury for our meeting with Italy's most glamorous side.

Early season training at London Colney. England against Ireland. Malcolm MacDonald and Alan Hudson this side of the net. Liam Brady, me and Frank Stapleton the other side.

John Devine was keeping Pat Rice out of the team so I was made captain that night. The game had been going no more than 20 minutes when Roberto Bettega went straight over the top at me. My shin is still scarred from his challenge. In fact, my shin pad was snapped in half, I needed stitching, and I watched the rest of the match from the directors' box.

He should have been sent sent off. The crowd went wild, booing him every time he touched the ball. As so often happens, somebody else was made to suffer for Bettega's cruel act. Marco Tardelli was sent off for the first tackle he made. Even in my anger and pain I felt sorry for him. As it was, Juventus scored first and good old Willie Young rescued us with an equaliser near the end.

I was disappointed in Bettega. I felt that what he did was out of character. It didn't help that he didn't ask how I was or apologise afterwards. Terry Neill went to town, calling Bettega a disgrace to his profession. I have always looked back on what happened as the worst tackle ever made against me. It wasn't late. It was calculated and right over the top. I was lucky to get away without a broken leg. My big worry now was that we had an FA Cup semi-final with Liverpool coming up on the Saturday. The immediate order was for me to get as much rest as possible. I spent the next day, Thursday, in bed.

The FA Cup semi-final was being played at Hillsborough. We were leaving on the Friday. I went into Highbury, but didn't train. I just had a walk round the pitch. A decision on whether I played would be made on the Saturday morning in Sheffield. Terry and Don wanted me to play. I knew it was a risk, but after breakfast in the hotel it was decided to take the chance. I was lucky. While my leg was very sore, there was no damage to the bone. When we got to Hillsborough, Liverpool's Phil Thompson was standing at the players' entrance. He asked, "Are you playing?" I didn't reply. Terry and Don wanted to keep them guessing.

It was early in April, and what followed was a tense, hard match. Brian Talbot hit the bar in the second half, but two good sides cancelled each other out and the result was a goalless draw.

Four days later, on 16 April, we replayed at Villa Park. This one finished 1-1, with Sunderland getting our goal. They scored first and we played some excellent football before Sundy equalised. It stayed 1-1 in extra-time and it was a better game then the first one. I got through it after a pain-killing injection before the kick-off.

On the Saturday, it was back to the League. We were in the top three but accepted that the Cups were now our best hope for a trophy, or perhaps two. So who did we meet on the 19th in the League? Liverpool! It was a bit ironic. They were top of the table and needed to win to keep up their League and Cup challenge. The match was at Anfield, it was another fabulous encounter, and we drew 1-1. We were well pleased.

I played, and I still don't know how I got through the game. We came back to London and had Sunday off, training at London Colney on the Monday morning before flying out to Turin in the afternoon. We based ourselves in the little town of Asti to prepare for the second leg. Soon after we had checked into the hotel that was to be our headquarters, I looked out of my bedroom window, and who should be walking up the drive but Bettega, with a television crew. Terry, I understand, told him to clear off. That evening, we gathered in the dining room for a meal, and Terry kept everything relaxed by saying we could have wine. Nobody took any liberties.

The following morning we went to train at the big stadium Juventus share with Torino. I made the journey with the rest of the squad, though Terry said it would be better if I just watched. I saw plenty of banners with my name on. I couldn't understand what they said, but I don't think it was too complimentary.

On the morning of the game, we did some light training next to the hotel and slept in the afternoon. The kick-off was at eight p.m. and we got to the stadium 90 minutes before the game. It was packed. Bettega tried to shake hands with me as we walked on to the pitch. 'Chippy' said, "Don't get involved."

They only needed a goalless draw after the 1-1 result at

Highbury. Typically, it was what they played for. We attacked from the start because we had to win. Fifteen minutes from time, Terry took off David Price and Brian Talbot and put on John Hollins and Paul Vaessen. Five minutes from the end the stadium became a sea of black-and-white Juventus flags. Their fans were convinced it was all over. There were just two minutes to go when Rix crossed to the far post and Vaessen scored with a stunning header. The silence was deafening. We made more noise celebrating.

I still didn't shake Bettega's hand. We were in the final. They had paid for not going out and trying to win. Later, we all went into the Juventus dressing-room to exchange jerseys. Tardelli, so unlucky to be sent off in the first leg, wished us all the best in the final. He was a player and a man for whom I had the greatest respect. Back at the hotel, we celebrated in style. I can still picture Holly speeding down the corridor on a moped.

We had to play West Bromich Albion next in the League on the Saturday. Terry and Don agreed to leave me out of this one. They were thinking about the third encounter with Liverpool on the coming Monday. We drew 1-1 with Albion, but the important thing was that we didn't pick up any injuries.

We travelled up to Birmingham on the Sunday for the game at Villa Park. It finished as another 1-1 draw. We scored after just two minutes through Alan Sunderland and held on until virtually the last kick of the game, when Liverpool equalised. Once more, it was extra-time. They attacked for most of the 30 minutes, but we held out. We travelled back to London late on Monday night steeling ourselves for the next attempt to settle this marathon tie . . . at Coventry on the coming Thursday.

The following evening, Pat Jennings, his wife, Joy and I went to see Johnny Mathis in concert at Wembley. Joy remarked that I looked a bit tired. She had to be kidding!

We travelled up to Coventry on the Wednesday afternoon. We were getting a bit used to that motorway. The third replay was on 1 May and the Cup final was only ten days away. There was already talk about the possibility of having to put back the final. It wasn't necessary. We won at Coventry 1-0.

Don gave an inspired and passionate team talk before the match, stressing, "We are stronger than them. We can do it. If we lift ourselves, if we believe in ourselves, we will go to Wembley." Brian Talbot scored with a header in the first half. It was enough. We were at Wembley for the third successive season.

We had two important League games before the Wembley final. The first was back to Coventry, where we won 1-0. Terry left out six of the Cup side – Jennings, Brady, Stapleton, Rix, Devine and me. We had Sunday off then played Notts Forest at Highbury on the Monday before Wembley. We drew 0-0. It suited everyone. They were in the European Cup final and didn't want any injuries. Neither did we. Tuesday was a day off and we came into Highbury on the Wednesday for a soak and a chat.

Thursday was spent at Colney, and it was there that Terry and Don made their decision. The big question all week was who would fill the left-back spot against West Ham – John Devine or Sammy Nelson. They were good friends and one of them was going to be disappointed. It was a hard decision for Terry and Don to make. They opted for John, with Sammy as substitute. I thought that making a full-back sub was a mistake, sorry as I felt for Sammy. In fact, he came on for John in the second half at Wembley, but it was a full-back for a full-back. Utterly pointless.

We had reached Wembley again. But somehow everything seemed flat. Frankly, we were all shattered. The season had caught up with us. I have a video recording of that final, but I have never watched it. Trevor Brooking scored for West Ham with a header in the first half and we lost a poor final 1-0.

At half-time, Don came into the dressing-room and ordered "Get yourselves under the showers. For God's sake wake yourselves up." It was no good. We were gone. I believe if we had played West Ham another ten times that season we would have won nine of them. I picked up a calf strain and didn't go on the losers' lap of honour. I felt it more important to get some ice on the calf.

We were leaving for Brussels and the Cup Winners' Cup final with Valencia on the Monday afternoon. We trained in the morning, but I was on the treatment table. On the Tuesday we trained at the Heysel Stadium, later to be the scene of such tragic events at a European Cup final, and the pitch was superb. Again, I didn't train. I had a work-out on the Wednesday morning and needed another pain-killing injection before the match. I knew, whatever happened, this would be my last game of the season.

My job that night was to stay tight on Mario Kempes. I like to think I did it well. There was no score after 90 minutes, and still no score at the end of extra-time. It was now down to penalties. It is a matter for the record that Liam Brady missed from the spot and so did Graham Rix. West Ham had beaten us in the FA Cup final . . . now Valencia had defeated us in the Cup Winners' Cup. It was hard to take.

It was also amazing how history had repeated itself. We had started that season by losing to Ajax in a tournament in Amsterdam. The game had been decided by a penalty shoot-out. Liam and Graham missed that night too. So the season ended the way it had started.

Well, not quite. We came back from Brussels, and it was "See you at London Colney". We still had two League fixtures to play – at Wolves that Friday night and at Middlesboro' the following Monday. We needed to win those games to claim the last remaining UEFA Cup place. We scrambled a 2-1 victory at Molineux and prepared for the very last lap of the longest season.

We flew to the North East on the Monday – from Luton in an old DC6. Sammy reckoned the plane needed a push to get it off the ground. It took nearly two hours to get to Middlesbrough. I don't think we got above 6,000 ft.

The game itself passed us by. The team, minus me, went through the motions. We were hammered 5-0 and it was goodbye Europe. Everyone was totally drained. Don came into the dressing-room afterwards and said, "We've had a tremendous year. We've won nothing, but we've still got a heck of a lot to celebrate on the way home. Well done every one of you.''

Besides reaching the finals of the FA Cup and Cup Winners' Cup, we got to the quarter-finals of the League Cup and finished fourth in the First Division. So near – and yet so far.

Everyone had a bottle of champagne on the flight back to Luton. Denis Hill-Wood, the chairman, had conjured them from somewhere, and he did his best to lift everyone's spirits. Yet it was impossible to keep a certain sadness out of that journey. We all realised 'Chippy' had played his last game for Arsenal. Whatever the club said, his contract was up and he was determined to take his talent abroad. From 5 April, when we met Southampton, to 19 May, when we played at Middlesboro' we took part in 16 important games in 44 days . . . eight in the League, five in the FA Cup, and three in Europe. There was no end-of-season tour. We didn't have the strength left.

CHAPTER NINE

Foreign Stars

Diego Maradona was 18 when I played against him in Dublin in 1979, the year after Argentina won the World Cup. Since then, for club and country, I reckon I have played against the rest of the best. Maradona remains the best.

In England, at that time, he was totally unknown. His "Hand of God" goal that helped knock Bobby Robson's team out of the 1986 Mexico World Cup was something for the far distant future. But we had heard whispers before that Dublin match against the World Cup holders that they had a kid who was something special, a youngster who was potentially better than any of their stars of that '78 triumph.

It was May, and the end of a long, hard season for me. Maradona came on in the second half. He was fantastic. Quick, with beautiful balance. And he was as strong as a bull, even at at that early age.

One little bit of magic I remember vividly. A ball came across from the wing and we both went for it. Maradona shaped to shoot, but instead chipped the ball past me on one side, went the other way, and hit a shot of venomous power. He didn't score – in fact the game ended as a goalless draw –

but it still left me knowing I had tangled with a genuine world star of the future.

Then there is Karl-Heinz Rummenigge. I first played against the fair-haired West German just before that meeting with Maradona, also in Dublin, and a couple of weeks after our 1979 FA Cup final win over Manchester United. He scored a goal that remains one of the best I have ever seen . . . coming on to the ball on the edge of the penalty box and placing it perfectly – almost passing the ball with uncanny accuracy into the net.

Rummenigge is big and strong, with legs like tree trunks and a willingness to run and battle all day and night. I admire him tremendously. His job was to score goals and he did it superbly.

Mario Kempes, of Argentina, is another who figures high on my list of outstanding foreigners – strikers I would rather play with than against. He proved his quality in the '78 World

That's me (second from the right) with the Republic of Ireland Squad in Moscow before we played the Soviet Union.

Cup. I fared better against Kempes than I did against Rummenigge. But I still rated him. He had a long, deceptive stride, excellent close control and a lethal left foot.

Roberto Bettega, of Italy, nearly broke my leg in one of our three meetings. It didn't make him my favourite foreigner. I never ever questioned his talent, though. He had a great first touch and the ability to get other players into finishing positions in and around the 18-yard box. Bettega had remarkable balance for a big man and held his line together in a way that always had you under pressure.

Another West German, Rudi Voeller, has always impressed me. He was with Werder Bremen, before going to Roma and the rich rewards of the Italian League, when I first came up against him. He is a mean finisher, always wanting to score and prepared to get hurt if he smells the remotest chance of a goal. Strength, particularly in his running, is a key part of Voeller's game.

I have played against the Dutchman Ruud Gullit several times – four of those occasions at international level. In terms of marking and trying to pin him down, I put Gullit in the Maradona class. He is a splendid all-round player, good in the air, brave and a sharp finisher.

Jan Ceullamans, of Belgium, is big, gangling and awkward but another great player. He shields the ball well and makes it very difficult for defenders.

I have played against the great Russian, Oleg Blokhin, twice – both times for the Republic. He is strong, quick and skilful, though not a very good team player. Without understanding a word he said, I soon realised he is a moaner, always arguing with his team-mates when the service wasn't right or they didn't react quickly enough to what he was trying to do. He always gave the impression he was right and they were always wrong. You could rough up Blokhin. But if you let him come and attack you with the ball, he is dynamite.

As a pair, and I have always believed the best strikers hunt in pairs, the Danes Preben Elkjar and Michael Laudrup are a bit special. While Elkjar is a terrific target man, someone it is hellishly difficult to shake off the ball, Laudrup's strength is his willingness to take on defenders in tight situations. He will dribble you in the 18-yard box. I have always been thought of as being pretty quick, but Laudrup is something else when it comes to pace. I had to dive on the Dane to stop him in one game.

If we could get players of the class I have mentioned into our league, it would generate excitement, fresh interest and a bit of extra variety. Yet, if I were a manager, I would think very carefully about taking a player from another country. Ossie Ardiles, at Tottenham, and the Dutch pair Arnold Muhren and Frans Thyssen, with Ipswich, can be put up as special examples of men who prove wrong my belief that foreigners generally struggle in the English League.

Nowhere else in the world do they play the number of games that we do. And there are no easy ones. Every match is highly competitive and the pace is usually blistering. Where else do they play four games in ten days, the way we do over the Christmas period? It is close, now, to being an 11-month season for English League players.

Because we play far too many matches, there is no time for managers and coaches to work with players at their skills. Most managers see strength, fitness and aggression as essential qualities. We breed and encourage players who can run and chase for 90 minutes without ever taking a breather, standing back, perhaps putting their foot on the ball and thinking about what they are trying to do.

I firmly believe it was this attitude that drove Glenn Hoddle abroad. I feel he got tired of the knockers, those people who brushed aside his breathtaking skill and attacked him for not getting in his quota of tackles. It leaves me with a feeling of despair that he has drifted on and off the world stage at international level. Nobody ever asked Michel Platini to play the way so many want Hoddle to. I think the treatment of Hoddle in this country was shameful.

Arsenal, in my time, have always been reluctant to take players from abroad. They were serious contenders for that outstanding Dutchman Rudi Krol, but nothing came of it. Vladimir Petrovic, a very good Yugoslav midfield player, did have a spell at Highbury, but he couldn't cope with the physical side of the game in this country and did not stay long. I thought it right for Arsenal to let him go.

Originally Terry Neill was going to pay around £350,000 for Petrovic. The Yugoslav Football Association stopped the deal and when he eventually joined us it was for a lot less. Arsenal were lucky. Petrovic made his debut against Swansea on 1 January 1983. Swansea gave him room to play and his display was stunning. But the good sides found him out, closed him down, worked on him. He couldn't cope.

It was said he suffered from not getting the right sort of support. But we couldn't afford to play the ball to him, then see him caught in possession. He just didn't like being tight-marked, hustled and harried. He could never understand why he was not allowed the freedom to express his unquestioned skill. Another game where he really shone was against West Ham at Upton Park when we won 3-1. He was outstanding. But it was 10 May, an end-of-season match with no pressure, and West Ham let him play. Yet I think we were all sorry it did not work out for Vladdy. He was very popular with the other players.

I have seen lads come down from the North of England and struggle to cope with the fast pace of life in London. I have known players get lost on the way to our training ground after a year at the club. Petrovic, after a couple of weeks, knew his way around better than most of us. He loved London, and enjoyed finding his way around on the underground and exploring the city. We missed him when he left.

For me, Ossie Ardiles has been by far the best of the foreign players who have come here to play in the Football League. I have always thought of him as being world-class. He makes things happen. He wants the ball and he has always been prepared to go and get it himself. I always rated Ardiles a superbly accurate passer of the ball over 15 yards. He wouldn't kill you with a 30-yard pass like Glenn Hoddle. But when he gave it, he always put himself in a position to get it back. He made people around him play. And after seeming to suffer initially from the pace of the game in the First Division, he worked at making himself stronger and fitter.

The one thing I have never liked about Ossie is the way he plays on referees. He is always moaning to them, playing for free kicks. In the early days, when referees had a go at him, he would give the impression that he didn't understand what they were saying. I don't believe that. It was one reason why he was never popular with our players. He also had this habit, whenever a free kick was awarded in his favour, of throwing the ball forward ten or 15 yards.

Ricky Villa, with the probable exception of that memorable double strike against Manchester City in the FA Cup final replay at Wembley, never made quite the same impression for Tottenham as his Argentinian pal. But Villa could certainly look after himself.

We played Spurs at Highbury in April 1979 and won 1-0. We nicked a goal through Frank Stapleton near the end and didn't deserve to win. During that match, though, I jumped for a ball with Villa and he coldly and deliberately put an elbow across my face. I was furious. Later, a ball was played up to him and, just as deliberately, I kicked him. We called it quits after that.

Frankly, Villa never appeared to have the same commitment as Ardiles. It was often suggested that he was little Ossie's 'minder'. But Ardiles didn't need a 'minder'. He could look after himself. He had a great awareness when the boots were flying. Ossie was a bit like Johnny Giles. He had a sixth sense when the tackles were coming in high and that little bit late.

The Dutch masters, Muhren and Thyssen, come next in my book among the men from abroad who successfully made the transition from their own country to the toughest league in Europe. I always felt, however, that Muhren was that bit more effective than Thyssen. Muhren had a cultured left foot, rather in the Kevin Sheedy mould. I always felt there was a great similarity between them.

David Pleat, when he was manager at Tottenham, paid what I believe was £600,000 for the Belgium international striker Nico Claessen. It was a mistake. At that time he could probably have got Mick Harford for the same money. Harford would have blended much better with Clive Allen. But Allen and Claessen didn't go together – something Pleat soon discovered. I don't think he did his homework very well.

Claessen is an out-and-out striker. He is quick and he can look after himself for a little fellow, but he needs to play off a target man and Tottenham at the time didn't have one. Claessen and Harford – or Allen and Harford – would be the perfect pairing. I admit to being a Harford fan. There are not many better all-round strikers.

Jesper Olsen, the Dane who made his home at Manchester United, I always compare him to Petrovic when he was at Arsenal. He is not suited to our game. The physical demands are too much for him. If you were aggressive with Jesper, he didn't want to know. He could be sensational one week and you would not see him the next week. He looked a star in Denmark's team of stars at the time of the Mexico World Cup. I could understand why United signed him. But he has never really produced the consistency that a club like United must demand in the search for honours.

Dutchman Johnny Metgod, like Claessen, made a mistake in joining Tottenham. He was a good player for Nottingham Forest in midfield. He always impressed me with the power he packed into his shooting. But Metgod followed Glenn Hoddle at Spurs – and he was never going to be another Hoddle. While he did well in midfield at Forest, I would say sweeper was his most effective position. I feel sure he regretted leaving Nottingham.

Mirandinha became the first Brazilian star to play in our League when Newcastle signed him. He is quick and will shoot from any angle if there is the chance of a goal. He didn't do badly last season, but I would still question whether Newcastle spent their money wisely. It was a gamble. He couldn't speak English. Newcastle got all that money for Peter Beardsley and it could have been spent on a player who was already established in the English game.

For a while at Liverpool, Jan Molby seemed to have a bit of a weight problem. For all that, he is a big, strong player who is a superb striker of the ball. He suffered from being injured. At Liverpool, with their enviable strength in depth, injury is something you just cannot afford. They say it is easier to get into Liverpool's side . . . than get back in.

West Ham's dabble on the Continent brought Belgium's Francois van der Elst to Upton Park. It was a brief flirtation. He was another who was unable to come to terms with the physical demands.

It is only when they come to play here that the stars from other lands realise the pressures on players in the Football League, with a variety of Cup competitions coming on top of a heavy League programme. The majority of the players who turn out game after game are probably carrying a knock of one sort or another. A lot of us go out to play accepting we are less than a hundred per cent fit.

CHAPTER TEN

Giles – The Best

Johnny Giles was manager of the Republic of Ireland side when I won my first cap 12 years ago. At international level, he was the best.

I was 18 at the time, still very much with 'L' plates on as a First Division footballer, when John picked me to play against England at Wembley. It was the game in which my Arsenal team-mate, Charlie George, made his one and only appearance for England.

The pressure on Charlie was far greater than it was on me. It would not have been helped either by what Giles had to say about Don Revie – then England manager. Giles, like all Revie's Leeds players, had the greatest respect for the man who legged it to the desert after walking out on England. But he knew, from long experience, Revie's weak points – and he punched them home to us before that Wembley game. "Don will be panicking like hell," he said. "All the England players will have their dossiers and they will be thinking they are playing a team of supermen. Don, I promise, has made you all out to be the greatest . . . world-class, every one of you."

Giles, who had left Leeds for West Bromich Albion – following Don Howe into the job – was the Republic's player-manager. He knew what he wanted and he was a centre-half's dream. He liked everything built up from the back and he never tired of repeating, "Don't forget, you've got me in front of you, I'm always there."

He was a superbly accurate passer of the ball with both feet. He could pick out and find the man he wanted from 50 yards with no trouble at all. He would say to me, and mean it, "I'm always there to receive the ball, but don't give it if I've got more than three players on me."

Giles was a great one for using the half-time interval to maximum advantage. Basically, a manager has got little more than five minutes to put right things that have gone wrong in the first 45 minutes. Some of them rant and rave, trying to frighten you. There are others who haven't got a clue where or why it has gone wrong and even less idea how to put it right. Johnny Giles never wasted a second, never mind a minute, of that precious time.

We got together on the Sunday at a hotel just outside London for the midweek Wembley match with England. Giles

The chase in on. Ireland vs Wales, 26 March 1986. Was this my last game for the Republic?

didn't arrive until Tuesday because West Bromwich had a game the previous evening. The players had gone off to play nine holes of golf on the Monday afternoon. Johnny Giles wasn't supposed to know. When he arrived on the Tuesday morning, he innocently asked how the training had been going. Without thinking, I dropped everyone in it by saying, "I didn't do too badly on the golf course yesterday." I felt very sheepish. I realised right away that John wasn't pleased. Playing golf was not his idea of the way you should prepare for an international.

Everyone respected Gilesy. He didn't rule by fear. He didn't have favourites and he treated everyone with courtesy. More important than anything, he knew the game.

On the Tuesday, we all went up to Wembley to park the cars at the hotel we would be using on the day of the international. He made a point of saying to me, "Forget your age. Remember you are in because of your ability." He didn't try to complicate things either. "When you get the ball, use it sensibly," was all he said. It was enough.

The teams came out on the night of the match and I walked side by side with Charlie George. He was a cult figure when I joined Arsenal and the reception he got from the Wembley crowd was rapturous.

We drew 1-1. Gerry Daley equalised for us in the second half after Stuart Pearson had given England the lead. It was an excellent result for the Republic and the general opinion seemed to be that I hadn't disgraced myself or let anyone down.

My best game against England I have always felt, however, was in Dublin in October 1978. It was in the European championship and again we drew 1-1. I shouldn't really have played. In fact, I came off ten minutes from the end with a groin strain. Kevin Keegan was European Footballer of the Year at the time and I played him out of the game. Gilesy, when I came off, said in the dug-out, "You've got to give Keegan ten minutes to show he can play too. That's only fair." It was a compliment I treasure to this day.

Giles was a father figure to all the younger players. He

always used to say that he was at the end of his playing career and had very little to show for it except for a lot of good memories. "Don't make money your god," he would tell us. "But remember it is important. This is a short career."

It was a shock to me when Giles quit and went to Vancouver in the old North American Soccer League. I know he was getting a lot of stick back in Ireland. People had turned against the way he wanted us to play it from the back. The carping and the criticism were affecting his family and I think he felt it just wasn't worth that sort of aggravation any more.

They talk about the luck of the Irish, but not too much of it ever seemed to follow Johnny Giles – or Eoin Hand, who took over from him. In the qualifiers for the 1982 World Cup in Spain we finished on ten points in the same group as France and went out on goal difference. Northern Ireland got to Spain with seven points. England made it there on eight points.

Jack Charlton? The Republic went to West Germany this past summer for the European Championships – their first ever appearance in a major finals. England were beaten by that Ray Houghton goal, we failed narrowly to reach the semi-finals, and Jack was a hero. But Jack was lucky. We went to West Germany only because Scotland pulled off a shock win in Bulgaria at the last knockings.

The best Irish side I have ever played in was the one that so nearly got to Spain in the World Cup of '82. It was packed with quality players – men such as Frank Stapleton, Liam Brady and Mark Lawrenson. But the best Irish side of all time is probably the one that went to Germany last summer. It is incredible when you think that half the side were born outside the Republic.

Eoin Hand was a surprise choice, as far as the players were concerned, to follow Johnny Giles. He was a nice man but he wasn't an international manager. At the time he got the job he was in the wilderness, running Limerick. But he was in Ireland, and he was available. Perhaps it was what those good men of the committee wanted.

Certainly, we had a truly disastrous run under Eoin's

stewardship. He would have meetings at which he would say he wasn't worried about the mounting criticism directed at him in the Press. But it got to him in the end. The media made his life hell. His kids came in for abuse at school.

With Eoin, the whole thing was a game of football musical chairs. He changed the team and tactics game by game. There was never any continuity. You could be in the side for one match and not even in the squad next time. Eoin tried to accommodate everyone. He would play Mark Lawrenson at right-back just so that he could put Mick McCarthy alongside me in the middle of the defence. It was wrong. Nobody felt settled or happy with what was going on. He also took the Republic on tours that Johnny Giles would have rejected instantly.

For instance, at the time of the war with Argentina over the Falklands, Ireland went to South America to play Chile, Peru and Brazil. It was crazy. Most of the selected players pulled out with what were supposed to be injuries. But the bottom line was that the clubs didn't want them to go.

I was away on tour with Arsenal and was supposed to join the Irish squad in Rio. Arsenal had gone out ten days earlier and we were in Barbados when Ken Friar, the Arsenal secretary, called me to one side and said the club would prefer it if I didn't go. I didn't present too many objections in case they changed their minds!

Half the Irish team had British passports and it caused no end of problems. For instance, the squad had to catch a connecting flight in Buenos Aires at one stage of the tour. Michael Robinson told me he handed in his passport and wondered whether he was going to be taken in as a spy. I flew straight to London from Barbados, and from there went on to Canada to see my brother Pierce.

In fact, I saw Johnny Giles in Vancouver around that time. I had never seen him happier or more relaxed. I believe he would still be there now if the NASL had not folded. The League game in England didn't suit the way John wanted to play. He didn't like being told what to do by chairmen and directors. He was too much his own man.

Eoin needed the Irish job – Johnny Giles didn't. Having said that, the arrangement with Jack Charlton makes sense. There isn't enough work for a full-time manager in the Republic.

CHAPTER ELEVEN

The Captaincy

The day I officially became captain of Arsenal was one of the happiest of my life. It was an honour to match anything else I have achieved in football.

The day and the way I lost the job was something else. It left me with a certain bitterness and possibly a few other people were finding it hard to look at themselves in the mirror immediately afterwards.

Season 1980-81 had started with Pat Rice as captain of the club, but not in the team. John Devine was keeping him out. so I led the side for the first few matches. John was a mate of mine, but I had great respect for Pat, so it wasn't exactly an easy situation.

Late in October of that season, Pat moved on to Watford. It wasn't a surprise. He wanted first-team football and the feeling at Highbury then was that Devine would hold down the right-back spot for quite a few seasons. Most of us at the club, myself included, were sad to see Pat go. But it was a good move for him. He didn't need to uproot his family by moving house and he was the sort of player Graham Taylor, who was making his mark at Watford as a top quality manager, needed. As a captain, Pat was one of the best – a

Getting the better of Justin Fashanu when he was at Nottingham Forest.

natural leader with the ability to motivate all those around
him.

It was a Saturday morning when Terry called me to one side
and said he wanted me to be captain of Arsenal on an official
basis. We were up at South Herts Golf Club, where we still
go for our pre-match get-togethers. Terry said he wanted to
make an announcement at the team meeting in 20 minutes
time. I felt honoured and delighted – but I also pointed out
I was only 22 and a bit young for the job. He answered that
by saying I had been in the team for a good while, I had the
experience and he had no doubts about my ability to do the
job. So I agreed to take it on. But I made it clear that, unlike
Pat Rice, I wouldn't be a bawler and a shouter. As good a
captain as he was, there were times when I felt Pat shouted
for the sake of it. I reckoned I could lead by example.

Being captain of a club with all the traditions you associate
with Arsenal had to be something special. I was thrilled – and
to think I had arrived at Highbury as a nervous 15-year-old
just seven years earlier wondering and worrying whether I
would be good enough to make it as a professional footballer.
When I look back now, eight years on, I have to say I don't
think I got as much help as I might have done.

Perhaps Brian Talbot, with all his experience, John Hollins
or Willie Young, with his commanding presence, felt they
should have been handed the job. I got on very well with all
of them. But if they are honest with themselves they will admit
they gave me little help and no advice on how to be a better
captain.

It wasn't an easy time for the club, and perhaps I really was
too young. Liam Brady had departed to Italy and Juventus,
now Pat Rice had moved on, and there was no doubt the club
was going through a transitional period.

Nobody said anything out in the open, but I could tell the
doubts about my appointment were there. I even asked Don
whether he thought I was doing a good enough job. He said
he and Terry were totally satisfied. They were backing me all
the way.

The captaincy didn't carry any more money and really,

there were no perks. The real responsibility was on match days. Other than that, if Terry wanted something done, particularly charity work or visiting a sick child in hospital, he would come to me and ask if I would organise one or two of the players. I was the link between the manager's office and the dressing-room. I was also in charge of the players' lounge on match days – making sure tickets didn't get into the wrong hands. Every player is allocated two tickets. There were times when I felt getting admission to the lounge meant more than getting in to see the match. It was looked on as a status thing.

That season we finished third in the First Division – seven points behind Aston Villa, who were champions. Kenny Sansom was the most significant newcomer to the side. But it had been a bizarre start to the season. I was on holiday in Florida when I heard that we had signed Clive Allen for a million pounds. Clive was at the club when I got back, suntanned, fit and raring to go. We set off for Scotland and matches against Rangers and Aberdeen.

Frank Stapleton, Clive and Alan Sunderland were all played up front, and it was like a traffic jam. Our success had been built on a 4-4-2 system. Suddenly, it was 4-3-3 to accommodate Clive. Frank and Clive would have been a good pairing – but how could you leave out Sundy? To all of us it was pretty obvious it wouldn't work.

We came back from Aberdeen on the Sunday evening and Frank and I flew straight to Dublin to play in a testimonial on the Tuesday for Paddy Mulligan. We were due to leave on the Friday for a tour to Yugoslavia. Terry and Don came out to see the game in Dublin. Don dropped me off home when we returned to Heathrow and it was on the drive to North London that Don said he doubted whether Liam Brady would do very well in Italy. He would struggle, said Don, to cope with the man-to-man marking. Don wasn't often wrong. He was wrong about that.

We went to Belgrade for a four-club tournament, and again the formation of Frank, Clive and Sundy up front didn't look right. On our return, we went to train at Colney. We were there when Clive said he had to go. He had an appointment.

It was the last we saw of him. The next day, Kenny Sansom turned up from Crystal Palace. He had been swopped for Clive. So we lost a good forward, but we gained a great full-back. It was still most odd.

For me, the feeling persisted throughout the season that I didn't get the sort of help from the senior players that I have tried to give to Tony Adams since he became Arsenal captain.

We got knocked out of the FA Cup in the third round at Everton and Tottenham beat us in the fourth round of the League Cup. In March, we signed Peter Nicholas from Crystal Palace. He gave us a bit of much-needed steel in mid-field and had some fine games on the run-in to the end of the season. It was a season that ended on a promising enough note – but again with the air around Highbury full of doubt. My own contract was up, so was Frank Stapleton's. I signed, Frank left for Manchester United and we went into the next season after losing another top-class player.

Really, the warning signs were there. I was still captain in 1981-82, a season that started with Alan Sunderland and Brian McDermott up front. It is not a criticism of Brian to say that he was a boy still learning the game. It wasn't the sort of thing expected from a club as big and as powerful as Arsenal. It would not have happened at Liverpool. When they lost Ian Rush, they signed Peter Beardsley, John Barnes and John Aldridge. When they lost Graeme Souness, they went out and bought Jan Molby.

We finished fifth and qualified for Europe again but we were never in a challenging position for the League. We were short of quality players. In the UEFA Cup, we went out in the second round to unfancied and almost unknown Winterslag. McDermott and Paul Vaessen were our strikers in the second leg. They were just kids . . . still learning the game. The FA Cup saw us beaten 1-0 by Tottenham in the third round while Liverpool put us out in the fourth round of the Milk Cup. It was, to put it mildly, a pretty average season.

So was 1982-83. I was still captain as we finished tenth in the League and lost in the semi-finals of the FA Cup to Manchester United. They also beat us in the Milk Cup, while

Moscow Spartak, with the help of a superb display and a 5-2 win at Highbury, put us out of the UEFA Cup.

During the era of Terry and Don, we always had a practice match at Highbury between the first team and the reserves on the Thursday before the first League match of the season. Season 1983-84 followed the usual pattern. I came in at the end of the game, had a shower, and was told by Terry that he wanted to see me in his office. Don was there. Terry said he thought the captaincy was affecting my game and they were going to make Graham Rix skipper.

What hurt most was that I already knew. A friend, thinking I had been told, telephoned to say how sorry he was that I had lost the captaincy.

Frankly, I was bitterly disappointed. It genuinely hurt that, when I was called to the manager's office, I knew in my mind what it was all about. So, it appeared, did half the club.

I wasn't going to be able to convince them I was the best man for the job. They had made up their minds. But I certainly could not accept that being made captain had affected

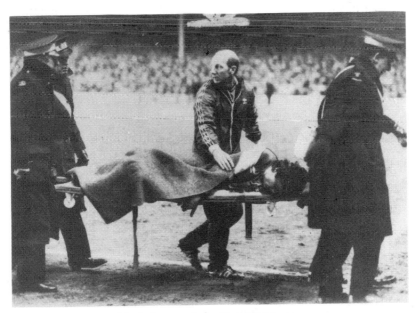

Me being carried off at Highbury.

my game. The team at the time wasn't right, and that made the captain's role doubly difficult. Sure, I made mistakes. But I was 22, and I feel now – as I did then – that I was too young, even though I had been in the side five years.

In all honesty, the club had become split. There were cliques. Certain players, I realised, were pleased I had lost the job. At the end of the 1982-83 season we had gone to Bali on tour. The squad were staying on for five days for a short break after the last game. I was coming home early because my son John had just been born and I wanted to be with him and my wife Joy. Pat Jennings told me later he had walked past one of the rooms where several of the other players were and he overheard one of them saying it might be a good thing to change the captain. Pat didn't say who the players were, but I had a pretty good idea.

The club by then had divided into two camps. In that situation, it didn't make things easy for me as captain. On one side, you had Tony Woodcock, Graham Rix, Kenny Sansom and Charlie Nicholas. In the other camp, you had Pat Jennings, Brian Talbot and Stewart Robson as the principal figures.

The two sides got on, but they were opposites in so many ways. It was known, even outside the club, that some players were going out socialising on Thursday nights – less than 48 hours before a game. Terry and Don called me in and said that as captain I should have a go at them. I felt very strongly that it was their job to do that. They were the manager and the coach. They had the power as well as the responsibility.

But I knew by then that certain players would not be unhappy to see me deposed as captain. In some ways, because of the undercurrent, I was glad to be out of the job. I have often wondered since whether certain players saw Terry and Don and let it be known they were in favour of a change in the captaincy.

We started the 1983-84 season by beating Luton and Wolves. Don said to me, "You're playing better." I think he was trying to suggest the captaincy had weighed me down.

I certainly felt Don influenced Terry to take the captaincy away from me and was influenced himself by an element inside the club. Perhaps he thought it would win them over. I know a lot of people could not understand the reasoning behind it. It particularly hurt that the decision had been taken, and became known outside the club, before I was told.

I came in on the day before the season opened and Graham said, "I'm sorry about what has happened. It came as a surprise." I couldn't help wondering just how big a surprise! My pal Pat said how sorry he was and how wrong he felt it was. They were sentiments repeated by Brian Talbot and Stewart Robson. I don't think 'Noddy' Talbot felt I was the greatest captain in the world, but it was clear he thought I had been badly treated.

When John Cartwright came to Arsenal as coach in 1985–86, after Terry had departed and Don was manager, he called us all together after a few weeks and said he felt there were cliques at the club. I know he wanted certain players out. But he didn't have the clout to get it done. He knew what was wrong at Arsenal and what was needed to get it right.

A lot of the players didn't agree with the way John wanted to do things. But he was very positive. What George Graham has done so successfully was very much what John wanted to do. He didn't have the power to push it through. He was fighting a losing battle against the cliques from the first week, and I think that, deep down, he knew it.

Pat Rice was much more outgoing than me. Whether he would have handled the situation any differently, I just don't know.

The best captain I have ever come across? Johnny Giles would definitely be right up there. Besides being an outstanding player, he had a great tactical awareness and the ability to put things right on the pitch as the game went on. He also had a will to win that rubbed off on others.

Steve Perryman, when he was at Tottenham, was another who always impressed me. He was a natural leader, also with a strong will to win. You always felt that losing never entered his thinking. He didn't shout a lot. When I heard him talking to his team-mates, it was always in a constructive way.

Martin Buchan, when he led Manchester United, was a

most impressive captain. He always seemed able to stay cool. What he said always seemed to make sense.

Graeme Souness was also a captain among captains – one of the very best. He played in midfield, which is a good position for a skipper. To say he was hard is an understatement. He was always in the thick of things, always dictating the play. When he did the business, so did Liverpool.

Time will tell whether Tony Adams, at Arsenal, can join the greats. I am delighted to say he has the potential. He knows he has my total support.

One last word about my time as Arsenal captain. One player, and it had nothing to do with my role as skipper, particularly disappointed me. The player was Tony Woodcock.

When the club bought Tony I thought it was a fantastic signing. He turned out to be the biggest let-down in all my years with Arsenal. He had done the business with Nottingham Forest and Cologne. He was a proven player. I had played against him and always found him a handful. But Tony never seemed able to cope with being an Arsenal player, living in London, and what that involved. He became part of the social scene, and I think his football suffered. It was a pity because he was so immensely talented. He should have been one of Arsenal's best buys – but we only saw his true quality in flashes.

CHAPTER TWELVE

Neill – The End

Terry Neill was sacked by Arsenal on 16 December 1984 – nine days before Christmas. There is no sentiment in football.

I have to say I was sorry to see him go. I must also say I was surprised. Having made those two points, I have to add that Terry, to a large extent, brought it on himself. In my view, the team and the squad had been allowed to run down. He had done nothing about it. Players had gone, they had not been adequately replaced, and what was left just wasn't good enough to compete at the top end of the market – where Arsenal have always got to be.

Yet season 1983-84 started on an optimistic enough note. Terry and Don Howe had signed new three-year contracts in the summer and Charlie Nicholas arrived as a big-money buy from Celtic in a deluge of publicity that suggested he was going to be the young man to lead us back to the good times.

Luton and Wolves were beaten comfortably enough in the opening two matches. But the opposition was not of the highest calibre and all those results did was paper over the cracks. Then, in the space of five days, Manchester United beat us 3-2 and we lost 2-0 to Liverpool. Both games were at Highbury. These were quality teams. Coming on top of a

defeat at Southampton, it didn't look good. Yet there was still
no indication of the storm clouds gathering overhead. Particularly as we then beat Notts County 4-0 away and Norwich
3-0 at home. It was roller-coaster stuff. We could beat the
also-rans, but the top teams were too good for us.

After losing to Queen's Park Rangers and Coventry Don
ran the legs off us at London Colney on the Monday. But it
wasn't lack of fitness that was our problem. We were just not
good enough. Deep down, I believe Don knew it.

The topsy-turvy stuff continued. We beat Nottingham
Forest 4-1 and won 6-2 at Aston Villa. We were up – then
down, following those wins by losing to Sunderland and
Ipswich before Everton were beaten 2-1. We got thrashed 3-0
by a poor Leicester team and Don had a go at all of us in the
dressing-room afterwards.

I was being partnered then at the heart of the defence by
Chris Whyte. It wasn't the best pairing. I had actually started
the season with Colin Hill alongside me and he wasn't even
a recognised central defender. I accepted I was awful at
Leicester. But I couldn't help thinking we were digging our
own graves.

Once again, when a player had left – in this case Willie
Young – he had not been replaced. Willie left Highbury in the
1981-82 season. It was now 1983-84 and the club had not
plugged the gap. It was the same with the right-back spot. Pat
Rice had been allowed to leave because it was felt John Devine
was the man for that position. But John failed to live up to
his earlier promise and was subsequently transferred to
Norwich. He was not replaced. Stewart Robson started the
season at right-back. He didn't want to play there. He thought
midfield was his best position and had the definite hump.

After that Leicester defeat, Tommy Caton was signed from
Manchester City for a reported £500,000. It had taken the club
two years to fill the gap left by Willie Young's departure.

On 29 November, three days after losing at Filbert Street,
little Walsall came to Highbury and beat us 2-1 in the Milk
Cup. Inevitably, there were comparisons with a more famous
Walsall Cup win over Arsenal several decades earlier. But the

implications and the repercussions were perhaps more serious for us this time.

This was the night the crowd's patience snapped. The fans were definitely on the turn. We sat in the dressing-room afterwards and could hear the chant ''Neill Out''.

Tommy Caton asked me later if Terry's job was safe. Terry didn't seem like a manager in trouble. On the surface he was chirpy enough, but I knew that he was feeling the pressure. I told Tommy I could not believe Arsenal would have let Terry spend £500,000 if they were about to sack him.

As usual, we had the following day – a Wednesday – off. The back pages of the papers were full of Arsenal crisis stories. The big stick was really out. This was crunch time for Terry. No doubt about that.

We came in on the Thursday, 1 December, and were told the chairman, Peter Hill-Wood, wanted to see the entire playing staff after training the following day – Friday. It was something that had never happened before in my entire time

I had the marks to show for this one. David Speedie tackles me in a game against Chelsea.

at the club. We finished training that Friday at about one o'clock. There was an hour to kill before the chairman's meeting so we all went to the fish and chip shop in nearby Blackstock Road to fill in the time before gathering again in the players' lounge back at Highbury.

Somehow, the Press had got knowledge of the meeting and the papers were all speculating about Terry's future at Arsenal . . . or lack of it. I heard Terry and Don talking. They were saying all the speculation wasn't helping. It was only adding to the pressure already on them.

Peter Hill-Wood, who had succeeded his late father as chairman at the start of the previous season, came in. I had the feeling that, if anything, he was embarrassed. David Dein, who had only just been appointed to the board, was with him. The chairman tried to make the point that, while he wasn't criticising us for lack of effort, he felt we were not giving one hundred per cent in the way of commitment. He said we were all on big money and probably earning a lot more than many people holding down top jobs in the City, where he worked.

Only the previous day, the chairman had gone on record in the *Daily Mail* as saying a lot of highly paid players at the club were not earning their salaries. Alan Sunderland, never slow to react to that sort of suggestion, had been simmering all day on the issue. He was not about to let the chairman's remark pass without a reply. He immediately jumped in and told the chairman he was out of order. He said he took it personally about players not earning their money.

Mr Hill-Wood didn't get the chance to answer. Terry Neill was up on his feet and saying to Alan, "You should take it personally. I'm dropping you against West Bromwich tomorrow."

The chairman's talk-in lasted 35 minutes. The recurring theme was that Arsenal, a giant of the game, should not be in the position they were in. Don said nothing. Sundy was the only player who spoke . . . and probably he wished he hadn't!

I felt the chairman was in an awkward position. I just couldn't see any point to the meeting. All it did was add to the pressure crushing down on all of us. However, I do accept that, at that time, not every player could put his hand on his heart and truthfully say he was showing enough pride in being an Arsenal player.

Even though there were shortcomings in the side, we should not have been in the position we were in. And there were definitely shortcomings. For two years, in my opinion, the club had just marked time. We had gone along with players who were doing a decent job. But the ones who should have been bought to keep us in a challenging position had gone elsewhere.

We met up, as usual on a match day, at South Herts Golf Club the following morning and there was not a lot left to say. Alan Sunderland was dropped and Tommy Caton came in for Chris Whyte. It was his debut, and in the situation we were in I didn't envy him. I had been injured in the débacle against Walsall, so Tony Adams took my place. Yet what really summed it up was two other changes. Dave Madden came into the side . . . so did Ian Allinson. Madden had been taken on a free transfer from Southampton. Allinson had arrived at Highbury on a 'free' from Colchester. No disrespect to either player – but this was Arsenal!

We lost 1-0. There were major demonstrations in Avenell Road outside the ground. What happened after the Walsall game was tame compared to this. The whole thing was escalating out of control.

Terry's only words after the game were "We'll put it right." He and Don both looked worried men. Terry knew the tide of feeling and opinion against him now might be impossible to reverse. To Tommy Caton, what we were seeing was nothing new. He said he had gone through it all before at Manchester City.

Arsenal's problems at the time were compounded of several factors. The club, as I have said before, had become one of factions. It didn't help that the dressing-room was split virtually into two camps. And the first-team squad obviously wasn't good enough. We were well short of the quality Liverpool and Manchester United could call on. Caton had been signed, but two years too late – and other positions now needed strengthening. The spirit of togetherness any club needs when things go wrong just wasn't there. There was tension about the place, and you felt some of the very talented players at Highbury were going through the motions – just biding their time.

On the Sunday, the newspapers, inevitably, were full of crisis talk. All the players were being asked by the media if we thought Terry was about to be sacked. The club was at a low ebb, with nobody, or so it seemed, knowing which direction we should now take. We had drifted along, and it had come to this.

Terry, I am afraid, had a lot to answer for. Willie Young, Steve Walford, John Devine, Steve Gatting, Pat Rice and Sammy Nelson had all gone from Highbury. I am not saying that the time wasn't right to let them leave. I am saying they were not adequately replaced. Kenny Sansom, before the arrival of Caton, was the only major signing in that time . . . if you accept he was swopped for Clive Allen, whose stay had been so brief and so pointless.

When we came in for training on the Monday, the sole topic for conversation among the players was whether Terry would survive the week. To the outsider, that probably seems harsh when you consider all the good times we had enjoyed together. But football is like that. What you did yesterday is quickly forgotten when things go wrong. I still felt Terry had a reasonable chance of riding the storm – simply because he and Don had been rewarded with new contracts in the summer.

Nothing happened. We worked hard in training, Saturday came, and we went to West Ham and lost 3-1.

The following Tuesday Graham Rix said to me he thought something would happen by the end of the week. A few days later, on the Friday morning, I drove to the ground for training, reached Highbury, and noticed that the chairman's car was outside. That was most unusual for a Friday. Obviously, something was happening. I walked into the club and there was a spooky atmosphere about the place. Tony Donnelly, the kit manager, said to me, "Terry has gone".

I've just scored. But it was only in a training match.

Don called all the players into the dressing-room and repeated what Tony had already told me. Don was to be in charge for the following day's home game with Watford . . . but we all reckoned he would eventually be on his way too.

I got stripped after training and Don came in and said, "What about that, son? Is that a joke?" I felt he was blaming the players for Terry's sacking. He added, "A good man has gone out of the door. You don't know who you will get here now. You will realise then what a decent man Terry was."

I accepted it as right the players should shoulder a proportion of the blame. But I felt the management had let things drift too. The team was split and it had been allowed to run down. I could not see Don getting the job. I felt it now needed a complete change at the top. After all, Don had been responsible for all the coaching. If he stayed, where were the new ideas to come from? And new ideas were needed just as much as new players. The club needed revitalising. And a new broom, I felt, was the only way that could happen.

We beat Watford 3-1, then went to Tottenham and beat them 4-2. Graham Rix was leading the lobby of praise for Don, saying he was the man for the job. Charlie Nicholas and Tony Woodcock joined the chorus. To be fair, they were all playing superbly and you couldn't knock the first couple of results following Terry's departure.

Yet the training hadn't changed, the tactics were the same. It was one of those times when two plus two were definitely not adding up to four.

The third round of the FA Cup came, we drew Middlesbrough away, and lost 3-2. We flew back from Teesside. I sat with Pat Jennings and Brian Talbot and all three of us agreed that defeat had cost Don the job. There was the no-poaching agreement among clubs concerning managers. We knew nothing could happen before the end of the season, but I was convinced the change would come in the summer.

Terry never did come back and say goodbye to the players. I telephoned him a week after his sacking and said I was sorry about what had happened. He thanked me and said, "There was a lot going on that you didn't know about. One day I will tell you.'' He never did.

Under Terry, Arsenal reached three FA Cup finals, a European final, an FA Cup semi-final and a Milk Cup semi-final. We always fininshed high in the League. His record was excellent. He was a first-class administrator. I believe if he had bought players when they were needed and not let the team run down he would still be manager of Arsenal.

A lot of the players thought he was a waffler. They also felt he made promises that were not kept. But I had no complaints. I have kept in touch with Terry. He doesn't live far from me and now and again he drops round for a coffee and a chat. I regard him as a friend and I believe he was a loss to the game when he left Arsenal.

I also know that Terry was not a hard man. He certainly wasn't ruthless. I have come to realise you need that to stay in football any length of time as a manager.

CHAPTER THIRTEEN

Nicholas – The Wrong Move

Charlie Nicholas spent four-and-a-half years with Arsenal proving he was a great fellow. Never, in that time, did he prove to be a great player.

It was one of the saddest happenings, or rather non-happenings, in all my time at Highbury. Through the managerial eras of Terry Neill, who signed Charlie, Don Howe, who followed, and George Graham, who finally sold him, Charlie didn't get past the stage of being Arsenal's 'nearly man'. In those four-and-a-half years he made countless friends. The North Bank, possibly desperate for a new hero, idolised him. Everyone at the club wanted him to do well. Somehow, Charlie never got near the winning post.

We were on one of those end-of-season tours, this time to Indonesia, which was pretty awful. We finished with a rather pleasant few days' break in Bali. That was where the players heard Charlie was coming to Arsenal.

There was a telephone call from London. Most of us were sitting round the pool when Terry came back to announce, "We have signed Charlie Nicholas." He and Don Howe seemed delighted. We all knew Liverpool and Manchester United had been in the hunt for Nicholas and I think the players were as excited as the boss. The immediate impression was that it was a great coup for Arsenal.

The fee, we heard, was £750,000. There had been a buzz for a few weeks that Charlie would be leaving Celtic and we were one of the clubs chasing him. I thought all along that he would go to Liverpool – until Terry's surprise announcement.

Ironically, Charlie always had this thing about Kenny Dalglish. The manager who has done such fantastic things at Liverpool was the man Charlie most admired. It went back to the Celtic connection.

Charlie was 21 when he arrived at Arsenal. He was supposed to be the final piece in the jigsaw of a new revived, all-conquering side. I think, when I look back, that we all expected too much. We were looking for the finished, polished product. For a fearless striker who was going to get us going again. For a prolific scorer. Charlie wasn't any of those things. He was an amiable young man with immense potential and a lot still to learn.

Yet he came with the image of a superstar built around him. Certain people on the fringe of the game were only too happy

Happy days are back. We've just beaten Liverpool in the Littlewoods Cup final, 5 April 1987.

to feed off that image in the early days. Charlie, frankly, just couldn't live up to all the ballyhoo. Perhaps, deep down, he didn't even want to.

In Scotland, Charlie had built a heck of a reputation in the couple of years before he came to Highbury. There, he really had been a prolific scorer. But the Scottish League then wasn't as competitive as it is now. Goals in England, as Charlie was to discover, are a lot harder to come by. The marking is tighter, the pace is quicker. If he had continued his football education north of the border for a further season, perhaps even two, I think his impact on the English First Division might have been sensational.

As it was, I felt he had come to the wrong club. He should never have signed for Arsenal. If Charlie had gone to Liverpool, they would probably have been able to shield him, protect him better than Arsenal could at that time, build him up, let him find his way in the reserves. With us, that just wasn't possible. He had to produce the goals from the very start.

Really, Charlie needed us to help him. Instead, we were looking to him to help us. We had just been beaten in two semi-finals by Manchester United – in the Milk Cup and the FA Cup. We had finished tenth in the League that 1982–83 season. we felt we were not that far off being a very good side. But we badly needed a consistent goalscorer.

The first time I met Charlie was on 15 July 1983. It was the day he reported to Highbury at the start of pre-season training. It is an Arsenal tradition that we go to the ground rather than London Colney on the first day, to be weighed, get kitted out and have the club photograph taken. The media attention, all focusing on Charlie, was unbelievable.

From that very first day, Charlie was friendly, very outgoing and very likeable. In many ways, that didn't help him. He is a person who likes company, who likes to have people around him. He lived in a flat and he didn't want to be on his own. So he went clubbing. His agent in those early days didn't seem to object to the reputation of "Champagne Charlie" that was building up. It stuck with him. And it was a false image – even though I think he secretly didn't mind being thought of as a bit of a character.

With nearly all of the first-team squad being married men, it wasn't easy for Charlie to find the right company. Married men, after all, like in the main to go home in the evening . . . though he did become close to Graham Rix and Paul Mariner.

Yet whenever there was a call for one of the players to visit a sick child in hospital – and that happens a lot – Charlie would always be the first to volunteer. He did a lot of charity work that was never publicised and Charlie would have been annoyed if it had been. If there were 200 kids waiting with autograph books after a game, he wouldn't walk away until he had signed every one of them.

Charlie, even if he had been out on the town the night before, was also a brilliant trainer. One of the best I've ever known. The only time I can ever recall him being in trouble was when we went to play a friendly in the Middle East. Charlie missed the plane at Heathrow. There are players I know who would have said, "That's it", and not even bothered to make the journey. We were going via Paris on Air France. Charlie made his own way out on a British Airways flight – and got there about the same time as us. As a punishment, the club made him pay his own air fare. Charlie did it without complaint.

At one time there was a story going the rounds that Charlie had been involved in a dressing-room punch-up with Steve Williams. It was nonsense. I don't think Charlie ever had even a verbal punch-up with another player at Arsenal – never mind a physical one.

His big thing throughout his stay at Arsenal centred around playing up front as an out-and-out striker. He always believed it was the role he was bought to fill. He never tired of talking about the job that Dalglish did for Liverpool when he was just a player. But there was an important difference. Dalglish could look after himself. I have marked him often enough. I should know. Kenny was tough. He couldn't be intimidated. Charlie wasn't hard. He wanted defenders to be nice. To temper their tackles. The game in this country just isn't like that. Defenders got to know that if you roughed up Charlie he didn't like it.

Charlie knew that the late Jock Stein had always wanted him to go to Liverpool. Yet he liked Terry Neill. Terry was easy-going, while Don Howe was much harder, much more demanding. Even so, when Terry left Arsenal, Charlie was quite open about wanting Don to get the job – even though Don used to get on at him all the time. He actually left Charlie out of the side a few times when he took over. Charlie didn't once complain, whatever he felt deep down.

I suppose it started to go seriously wrong for Charlie when George Graham succeeded Don. George likes forwards who can hold the ball up and look after themselves. He is not a manager who expects players to concentrate on the physical side. But he does believe it is a man's game, and that when the ball is played up to the front men it has got to stay there – not come straight back.

Charlie got the two goals that won us the Littlewoods Cup towards the end of the 1986-87 season. But we all realised that was only a temporary stay of execution as far as Charlie was concerned. The boss always insisted it was a team effort that saw us through 2-1 over Liverpool at Wembley. He wasn't fooled or won over by that one game.

Before that, when Don Howe was still manager, he tried to get the best out of Charlie by using him behind a front two of Tony Woodcock and Paul Mariner. I always felt that wasn't the answer to the dilemna of how best to use Charlie. After all, the club had paid £750,000 for a scorer – not a provider.

From the very start of his managerial reign, George Graham wanted to play 4-4-2, with a target man and someone to play off him. There was no room for Charlie in that system. After losing his place following the first three games of season 1987-88, it was inevitable that depression did finally settle in on Charlie. It was sad. And we all felt for him. He had this terrific rapport with the fans. Yet he was nose-diving towards total obscurity. No player since Charlie George and later

Liam Brady had captured the Arsenal public's imagination the way Charlie Nicholas did.

The best spell he had at Arsenal was at the start of the 1984-85 season when for ten games he at last looked ready to realise that vast potential. We played Watford and then Newcastle early in September. We beat Watford 4-3, he scored twice and absolutely destroyed them. That was probably his best game for the club. I scored that day – but in the wrong net! It was my only goal of the season!

On the day Charlie left Arsenal to return to Scotland with Aberdeen we were training at London Colney. Charlie said goodbye to all the players individually. I was having a soak in the bath when he came in and said, "All the best, Paddy." I wished him the same and sincerely meant it. Charlie deserved a change of luck.

As far as I know, Charlie didn't say cheerio to the boss and the boss didn't say goodbye to him. The game can be like that.

CHAPTER FOURTEEN

Now Howe

Pat Jennings, 'Noddy' Talbot and I were all wrong about Don Howe.

He had taken over as caretaker manager against Watford on 17 December and when we went out of the FA Cup at Middlesbrough the following month, his chances of getting the job on a permanent basis appeared to be zero. In the dressing-room at Ayresome Park that day, Don had been very down afterwards.

We had a team meeting at Highbury the following Monday where Don said, "It's all about pride now. There is still a job to be done and we have all got to get on with it." He didn't say a word about wanting the manager's job. Even though his chances looked to be slim, we knew he still wanted it.

We tried to win as many games as we could . . . for our pride as much as Don's. The Saturday after the disaster at Middlesbrough we went to Luton and won 2-1. Then came the crunch. We played Queen's Park Rangers at Highbury. This was more than an ordinary First Division game. The media, understandably, built it up as a head-to-head confrontation between Don, the man in possession of the Arsenal manager's job – however temporarily – and Terry Venables, the man

*A lift into Europe?—Southampton's Mike Channon provides the base for
David O'Leary's Arsenal hopes.*

most likely to succeed him. Rangers beat us 2-0 and even our most fanatical fans would have been forced to admit they deserved to win.

In the players' lounge later, Rangers' Gary Waddock said to me, "There can't be much doubt about it now. Terry must be lined up for Highbury at the end of the season." All of us knew the match had meant a lot to Don. We had given one hundred per cent plus, but it wasn't enough.

On the car radio going home I listened to an interview with Terry Venables. He said nobody had approached him about the Arsenal job, and he thought Don Howe was the man for it anyway. That didn't sound like someone most of us reckoned would be our boss come next season.

It was interesting that, in February, Don bought Paul Mariner from Ipswich and he made his debut in a 1-1 home draw with Aston Villa. The board, I reasoned, wouldn't have let Don buy Mariner if they were going to sack him. But then I remembered Terry Neill, just before his dismissal, had paid out £500,000 for Tommy Caton.

We played Manchester United, lost 4-0, and Tommy was sent off. Just before that game we had gone to Marbella for a short break. It was a trip that met with the approval of a lot of the senior players.

On 21 April we beat Tottenham 3-2 at Highbury. A result like that – beating Spurs always came high on the season's list of achievements – couldn't have come at a better time for Don. The crowd were chanting "Don Howe for manager" and the Press were backing him too. I started to think the odds were now turning in his favour.

We beat Leicester 2-1 at home, and afterwards Don came into the dressing-room, went round and shook hands with everyone, and announced, "Thanks very much. I've got the job." I think we were all pleased for Don. It just seemed a bit of an anti-climax.

His record following Terry's departure was indeed impressive. Between Terry going and the end of the season our League record was won twelve, drew ten, lost three. That was championship form.

I don't to this day know whether Arsenal approached Terry Venables or anyone else to become manager. Or whether they realised they couldn't at that time get anyone with a pedigree better than Don. Or even whether the way the fans got behind Don forced them into something that deep down they possibly felt wasn't right. It could well be that they were left with no alternative.

I was delighted for Don. But I stick to my view that, when Terry went, it was time for a clean sweep of the backroom staff. Don said on the radio that he was never involved in the actual running of the team in Terry's time. I found that hard to believe. Don was such a powerful force on the training pitch that I cannot accept he had no say in the picking of the team. I was not alone either in that view after Don's radio interview.

It was a quiet summer. We were all waiting to see who Don would appoint as his right-hand man. Terry Burton had helped out in that role when Terry left. Now he was to get his chance as first-team coach on an official basis. The only real change on the coaching staff was to make up the numbers. That was done by promoting Tommy Coleman from youth to reserve team coach and bringing back Pat Rice from Watford to look after the youth side.

The day before we reported back for pre-season training, Viv Anderson was bought from Nottingham Forest for £250,000. It was a top-class signing, but again we were filling a position that had been a problem for too long.

We opened that season with a 1-1 draw against Chelsea. Our first midweek match was at Nottingham Forest. It was their opening home game. I remember Brian Clough writing in the programme, "We wish Viv Anderson all the best with his new club and welcome back Tony Woodcock. If I was a betting man I would say the phone line between the Anderson and Woodcock homes was red hot during the summer." We lost 2-0.

We finished seventh in the League, and it was a far from memorable season. We lost at York City in the FA Cup and at Oxford United in the Milk Cup. Pat Jennings had a badly swollen thumb that night at Oxford and should never have played. Big Billy Hamilton had asked me during the game, "What's up with Pat?" I said, "He shouldn't be playing."

John Lukic had travelled with the team to Oxford, but he was reckoned to have an injury too. Don said in the dressing-room to Pat afterwards, "Their winner was down to you. You made a mistake. But you'll bounce back."

We went to Manchester United for a live television match on the Friday night and lost 4-2. Lukic was fit to play in that one.

Sheffield Wednesday at Hillsborough was our next live appearance on the telly. This time it was ITV and on a Sunday. We lost 2-1. During shooting-in practice the Friday before I hit a shot and pulled a thigh muscle. Ten minutes into the second half I had to come off. I sat on the bench to watch the rest of the game.

Roy Johnson, who had followed Fred Street as Arsenal's physiotherapist when Fred went into private practice, liked to shout his mouth off during a game. He was always giving players stick. As I sat down in the dug-out, a cross came over and Pat Jennings was a bit slow going for it. Roy screamed, "Look at that, Don. He went for that ball like a sack of coal."

When we got back to London Colney to pick up our cars on the Sunday night, Pat had a go at Roy. The following Tuesday when we reported back for training, Pat took the matter up with Don. Don defended Roy, saying, "He is a member of my staff. I back him." Pat never played another first-team game for Arsenal . . . other than his farewell-to-football match against Tottenham. It had been a season to forget.

We reported back for a new season and the speculation started all over again. Would Don still be manager when the games got under way? My own view remained the same. Don should have gone a year earlier.

There was, however, one major change. We arrived for training on the first day to find John Cartwright, the former England Youth manager, installed as chief coach. Terry Burton had been relegated to the reserves. Tommy Coleman was out. Nobody knew John, but he came with good credentials. We were all asking . . . Would he be allowed to do the coaching?

Don, to be fair, gave John his chance. Like Terry when he was manager, Don would now stand on the edge of the pitch during training and make his points later. I found it strange. It just wasn't Don. His greatest strength was coaching . . . being in the thick of it with the players.

John was very positive about what he wanted. Quite simply, he wanted the ball played forward as quickly as possible. It would be channel balls and no compromise. I couldn't see the sense of that for one simple reason. Our front two were Tony Woodcock and Charlie Nicholas. They were players who needed it played to feet – not into the channels . Charlie, for one, just didn't have the pace for that sort of game. John had his reasons for the system, but we really didn't have the forwards to play it that way. We needed a big man up front. To be fair to John, I know he wanted Niall Quinn in the side from the very start but Don couldn't find a way to leave out Charlie or Woody.

John loved players with pace at the back. We were playing Liverpool, we had just lost 3-0 to Southampton, and by a mixture of accident and design John got what he wanted. Martin Keown came in for Tommy Caton at the back and, with Woody injured, Quinn finally got his chance up front. It worked a treat. Niall was outstanding. He worried Mark Lawrenson and Alan Hanson non-stop. I was in the bath afterwards when John came to me and said, "See the way it worked with Quinny." Niall was superb and scored in a 2-0 win.

The youngsters thought highly of John. Many of the senior players in the side didn't like him. For his part, I got the feeling John would not have been unhappy to see players such as Charlie, Woody and Graham Rix out of the side.

Don and John seemed to get on well. I found John a nice man, but I think he made enemies. He spoke the truth. He wasn't one to consider the implications before saying something. He told it as it was. He wasn't afraid to say what he felt was wrong with the club. Paul Davis and David Rocastle were players who thought very highly of John Cartwright. They respected the help and advice he gave them in helping them to be better players. Some of us thought John was entitled to more support than he got inside the club.

For me, the beginning of the end for Don as manager came when Luton beat us in the fifth round of the FA Cup in a second replay. I wasn't alone among the players in believing his number was up. In just over two seasons under Don we had won nothing and achieved little.

We were playing Aston Villa after going out of the Cup to Luton. Before the Villa game Don, as only he could, gave an inspired team talk . . . punching home the point, "Let's finish the season in style." The response was a 4-1 win over Villa followed by victories against Ipswich, West Ham, then Coventry. After Coventry had been thrashed 4-0 I had to dash to Heathrow to catch a plane to Dublin. The Republic of Ireland were playing Wales in Jack Charlton's first game as the Republic's manager.

We were playing Tottenham the following Saturday. No matter where we were in the League, that was always the big one. As I dashed away from Highbury, Don said to me, "All the best. I know you'll look after yourself. You don't need me to tell you it's Spurs next week. We want to win that one."

I was driving along the M4, heading for the airport. It was 5.45 and I had *Sports Report* on the radio. The presenter suddenly said, "We have a news flash. Don Howe has just resigned as manager of Arsenal." I was so shocked, by the timing more than anything, that I reckon I did well to keep the car on the road. I still don't know what happened in the 45 minutes between his wishing me luck in Dublin and the announcement of his resignation.

As I climbed aboard the plane for the flight to Dublin I would have bet my house on Terry Venables getting the job this time. The first thing I did when I returned from the international in Dublin was telephone Don and say I was shocked and sorry about what had happened. He didn't give me any explanation.

Don, it was said, was upset because he felt Terry Venables

Cycling helps me get back to full fitness after an injury.

had been approached about the job at Highbury while Don himself was still doing it. In fact, I believe the chairman tried to do things in a gentlemanly way . . . telling Don his contract would not be renewed at the end of the season. I believe that happened after the Luton Cup defeat.

Nobody could take away what Don had done for Arsenal. He was coach to Bertie Mee when Arsenal did the League and FA Cup double. As right-hand man to Terry Neill, he was a key figure when we appeared in three successive FA Cup finals. Possibly, he outstayed his welcome. Perhaps he should have been given his chance as manager a lot sooner.

But Don proved you can't keep a good man down. I was delighted last season when his coaching skills were largely responsible for little Wimbledon getting to Wembley and winning the FA Cup. They didn't need to show Don the way to the dressing-rooms. He had been there often enough.

There was a collection among the players to make Don a presentation when he quit Arsenal. We raised more than £200 and gave him some crystal cut glass. About a month after the Coventry match he came into Highbury after training one day and we made the presentation. There were no speeches. What was done was a mark of our respect for the man. Don just said, "Thanks," and that was it.

Chief scout Steve Burtenshaw took temporary command for the remaining 11 games, making it clear he didn't want the job. At the end of that season, I saw John Cartwright at the Football Writers' Association annual dinner. We got talking and he explained his decision to leave Arsenal at the same time as Don by saying, "What was the point in staying? I knew I was on a hiding to nothing once Don went." I'm not sure that didn't apply even when Don was there.

I have not seen John since, though he came to my testimonial match with his wife and wrote me a nice letter afterwards. Don phoned me before the game and wished me all the best, apologising for the fact that he wouldn't be able to be there. Terry Neill and his wife came to the game. Really, it was the end of an era.

All the talk as the season ended was who would be the new

master of Highbury. Terry Venables was the firm favourite. When he dropped out, Graham Taylor came very much into the frame. Tony Donnelly, our kit manager, was quietly saying all along, even when the Terry Venables hype was at its height, that George Graham was the man for the job. He was the one who got it right.

We played Chelsea in our last game of the season at Highbury on 29 April. George was at the match. It was the first time I had seen him at a home game. I saw him again at the Football Writers' dinner and I still don't know whether he knew that night that he was the next manager of Arsenal.

I have to say I never managed to get close to Don. But I appreciated his values. He was a great family man and he was absolutely straight. He was a nice man, and funny when he let his guard drop. But it was difficult to talk to him on any subject other than football.

Don was very strong on discipline. He was always wanting to fine players . . . particularly for being late. When Graham Rix appeared in Court on a drink driving charge, it cost him the Arsenal captaincy in Don's time as manager. Ironically, Graham probably got closer to Don than any other player. Don had a particularly high regard for Graham.

CHAPTER FIFTEEN

The Hill-Woods

I was 16 when I met Denis Hill-Wood for the first time. I knew he was the Arsenal chairman and I had come to learn that he was well liked by the senior players. But to me, at that time, he might just as well have been the man in the moon. Fourteen years ago, football club chairmen did not have the high profile that men such as Ken Bates, Irving Scholar and Martin Edwards have now.

At the end of a season it used to be Bertie Mee's custom, when he was manager, to give a first-team outing to a young lad who was showing promise in the reserves. It was a chance for the youngster to absorb the first-team atmosphere and for the coaches to assess his potential. This particular year it was my turn. Arsenal were playing a testimonial at Reading and Bertie put me in. I remember getting on the team bus at Southgate underground station and sitting next to Charlie George. Barry Hughes, who has spent so much time coaching in Holland, was there with Bertie. They were old friends.

I was in the dressing-room before the game when Bertie came in with Mr Hill-Wood and introduced me as "one for the future". The chairman wished me luck, said he hoped Bertie was right . . . and that I would come through. After the game, the chairman came into the dressing-room, saying to me, "Well done young man. You did really well." I was delighted.

We played at Reading in the FA Cup in season 1986-87 and it mentioned in the programme that Elm Park was the ground where I made my debut for Arsenal. The lads were all joking about Stanley Matthews and Tom Finney being in their prime at the time. I sat in the dressing-room and remembered that exact spot where the chairman had stood all those years ago.

He was a fine man . . . a chairman of the old school. He was always genuinely concerned about the welfare of the players and loved Arsenal. Whenever he saw me, he would always come over and have a chat. The other lads used to rib me afterwards, joking, "Is everything OK? Did he say anything about new contracts for us?" But it was all good natured.

Later, when I made my Republic of Ireland debut at Wembley against England, I was told the late chairman had

I gotta horse. Or at least my wife Joy has. His name is Secret.

come to the game specially to see Arsenal's Irish trio of Liam, Frank and myself.

We would be on tour or on a European trip and Ken Friar would be worried about getting everyone off to bed after the game so that there would be no mishaps the following morning. We would all be in the bar, including the chairman, who would say, "Ken, who is chairman of this club? You get off to bed. I'll look after the players. They won't come to any harm."

I remember when he got ill. Ken Friar said to me, "The chairman wouldn't mind you going down to see him." My contract at that time had six months to run and there was a lot of talk about whether I would sign a new one. Ken made it clear, "He won't talk about your contract."

I set off after training. Mr Hill-Wood lived down in Hampshire, in a beautiful part of the world. We had tea, talked for a long while – and not one word was said about my plans for the next season. The chairman, I knew, thought that was a matter for discussion with Terry Neill and Ken Friar – not him. I respected that.

There have been kings, counts and prime ministers as guests of other board members in the directors' box at Highbury. Fair enough. Arsenal, after all, are the most famous club in London – the natural place for football-loving dignitaries from the other countries to visit when they want to see a game. Denis Hill-Wood, however, would invite the landlord of his local pub or his gardener to games. And he would not let them feel out of it. He would introduce them all round in the boardroom afterwards.

I saw him a few days before he died. He looked very ill. Ken Friar came to me again and said the chairman was back in hospital and it would be nice if one of the players went to see him.

Ken drove me to the hospital after training. We were not having the best of times around then. Results were not good and the chairman said to me, "What the hell is happening to our team?" It was very sad. We stayed about 15 minutes. I wished him all the best, but I knew coming away that he had watched his beloved Arsenal for the last time. I would not see him again.

The funeral was private. But there was a memorial service some time later. Everyone in football seemed to be there . . . directors, managers, players. It was a mark of the respect in which he was held. If I had left Arsenal by then, I would still have gone to the service.

He was a terrific character. We once went up to Scotland to play a pre-season friendly with Celtic. We had lunch in Glasgow at the hotel opposite the airport. Mr Hill-Wood, I noticed, was having lunch with some other people. I said to him later, "Did you have a nice lunch, Mr Chairman?" He replied, "Yes, excellent. That was the Rangers' chairman and his board. I think they are a bit worried that I'm getting too friendly with Celtic. It doesn't do any harm to keep them on their toes."

Coming back from the Far East once, Terry Neill had issued the order there was to be no drinking on the plane. After a while, we all got a bit restless. The players were travelling in the economy section, while the chairman was upstairs in the first-class lounge of the 747 that was taking us all home. Mr Hill-Wood wanted to invite us all up for a drink. I explained that we couldn't . . . the manager had forbidden it. The chairman immediately called up Terry, and said to him, "We'll all have a drink." The problem was solved.

Mr Hill-Wood loved the club. He was particularly fond of players who were loyal to Arsenal. Some clubs, I know, give little or no help to players who have testimonial matches. That is not Arsenal's way. After one of these games, they always lay on a buffet. Following Sammy Nelson's match, Ken Friar asked Mr Hill-Wood, "How much do we deduct for the cost of the reception?" The chairman retorted, "What do you mean? We'll take care of the expenses." Sammy, in fact, always was one of his favourites.

Once, when we played Manchester United at Old Trafford, the chairman came into the dressing-room before the game and said to Terry, "The directors had lunch at a lovely hotel on the way up. Excellent restaurant. I think the team would

really like it. Let's think about it next time we play up here.''
Mr Hill-Wood was always thinking about the welfare of the
players . . . and what might please us.

He was very friendly with the late chairman of Ipswich,
John Cobbold. He used to look forward to going to Portman
Road. He told me once he stayed so late after a game, he got
locked in the ground. I think it was an afternoon match too!

The chairman would always come into the dressing-room
before a game and wish us luck. Afterwards he would put his
head round the door again to say, ''Well done'' or ''Hard
luck''. He rarely said more.

Peter always came with his father to the games. He didn't
say much in those days. Denis didn't like America. Peter got
married over there and I asked the chairman if he enjoyed the
wedding. He said, ''Yes, thank you'' – adding, ''I got there
the same day and came home the following day. I would have
come home the same day if I could have got a flight.'' He was
very English.

He was against advertisements round the ground as well as
sponsors' names on shirts. I don't know what he would think
of things now . . . whether he would have come to accept that
such things were an inevitable part of progress. I do know he
was a remarkable man – and football, as well as Arsenal, lost
one of the game's great chairmen when he died.

We played Liverpool at Highbury on 11 May 1982. It was
a night match and the memorial service for the late chairman
had been held that morning. There was a minute's silence
before the kick-off. There was a big crowd, and the fans
seemed to sense what Denis had meant to us all. You didn't
hear a cough or a whisper. You could feel the respect in the air.

It was inconceivable that anyone other than Peter would be
the next chairman. Peter, like his father, does not interfere in
team matters. That has got to be a bonus for an Arsenal
manager. Nor does he seem to be at the club as much as his
late father. He doesn't come to all the games. But when he is
at Highbury, Peter will always come in and say ''Hello'' to
the players.

Ken Friar has been on the board for several years now. He

started at Arsenal as an office boy and has gone on to become managing director. While George Graham is in complete and total charge of the playing side, Ken runs the rest of the club. You never see him in the dressing-room, and that is the way it should be. He is a top-class administrator – the best – and you know if he says 'Yes' to something, it is 'Yes'. If he says 'No' it is 'No'.

He has always given me good advice . . . emphasising the point once that a professional footballer's career does not go on for ever and that when a player is at the top he should invest his money in a good pension. He helped me with my testimonial and I was grateful.

The rest of Arsenal's directors tend to stay in the background, though David Dein, who is now vice-chairman, is rather more outgoing. Before he joined the board, I used to see quite a lot of him in the players' lounge as a guest of Willie Young.

I have met Tottenham's chairman, Irving Scholar, several times and he has impressed me as something of a football fanatic. If he sees you somewhere, he always goes out of his way to say "Hello" and have a chat. I like his enthusiasm.

When I met Ken Bates, of Chelsea, I found it easy to understand why he makes so many people bristle. You enter the directors' box at Stamford Bridge from the back and walk down the steps to the front. Once, when we played there, I wasn't fit. But the boss, George Graham, wanted me to come to the game and sit with him. Ken Bates was at the front on one side and we had the first two seats on the other side of the aisle. I was on the outside. Mr Bates looked at the programme, looked at me, and said, "Excuse me, Mr Quinn. According to my programme you are supposed to be out there playing." He knew who I was all right.

I came face to face with Maurice Rowarth, the Nottingham Forest chairman, in a most unusual way. We were playing Forest at Highbury and I got a bit of a knock. I walked out of our dressing-room to go to the treatment room and he was outside their dressing-room. He said, "Bad luck today. I hope your injury clears up." Brian Clough had locked him out of the Forest dressing-room and he was waiting patiently to be allowed in. And Forest had beaten us that day!

CHAPTER SIXTEEN

Hard Men and Hit Men

To the Brazilians, it is the beautiful game. To those of us who earn our living in the English league, it can be hard and occasionally brutal.

I have come to accept over the years that any team wanting to be successful in the First Division must have that necessary bit of steel. Usually, that means a hard man . . . a player able to sort out the opposition so that those around him can play. There are those who might disagree. They are burying their heads in the sand.

It is from the centre of midfield that the best of the hard men seem to operate. There were few better than Peter Storey. Midfield artists such as Arsenal's present manager George Graham, Alan Ball and later Alan Hudson were all able to express themselves that bit more freely because of the protection they got from Storey. We would walk out before a game and 'Snouty' Storey would deliberately look hard and long at the player on the other side it was reckoned might give us the most trouble. He had the coldest eyes I have ever seen.

Bobby Campbell, when he was coaching at Arsenal, had the first team playing the youth side one day. 'Snouty' came in for a shot on the edge of the penalty box and I stopped him with a block tackle. He gave me one of his famous looks. He didn't say a word. But the message was there . . . "Do that again, and you're in trouble."

I was 17 when I played at Stoke. Alan Ball was fiddling around in midfield when one of their players whacked him. Bally went for him. But 'Snouty' went over the top of Alan to get there first. Nobody took liberties with Arsenal when he was around.

There was a day, though, when Storey met his match. We were playing Leeds and Bertie Mee told Peter that Johnny Giles was the man who made it all happen for them. No more. Just that. The only problem was that Don Revie must have warned Giles that Storey would be looking for him. The game hadn't been going more than 20 minutes when Giles sorted out 'Snouty'. Giles was as hard as they come.

It saddened me, and most of us who knew him, that Peter ran into so many problems when he left football. I found him a very quiet man . . . a loner. When we played away, he would usually sit on his own at the back of the coach and read a book. Alan Ball was the only one who could get him to smile and be a bit outgoing. I always knew I would rather play with him than against him.

Johnny Giles always said to me that it was wrong to expect defenders to sort people out. His view, and I know it to be right, is that referees are always watching defenders. The men at the back get away with very little. When he was at Leeds, in the all-conquering Don Revie days, it was Giles himself and Billy Bremner who did the hard-man stuff.

There cannot be a fan anywhere in the country who does not admire Liverpool for the quality of their football. That army of admirers includes most of us who earn a living from the game. Yet Liverpool have always had their hard man. Tommy Smith, by any standards, was a bit special. We played them on one occasion and a ball was pushed down the line for Liam Brady. Tommy went for it at the same time as Liam and missed both him and the ball by inches. Such was the force of his challenge, he finished up

*Winning an aerial battle with Glenn Hoddle in his Tottenham testimonial at
White Hart Lane.*

in the dug-out. There were times when Smith made Peter Storey look like a choirboy.

Around that time, we met Liverpool in the semi-finals of the Milk Cup. Malcolm Macdonald was with us then. The day before the first leg at Anfield, Malcolm put his name to a signed article saying what he was going to do to Smith. We were staying at the same hotel Liverpool use on match days. At lunchtime on the day of the game we headed for the restaurant and the lift stopped a couple of floors below ours. Tommy Smith got in. He saw Malcolm, gave him a cold look, and said, "I've read your article. I hope you are going to keep your word." Malcolm stayed well away from him that night.

Tommy could play, but he didn't take nonsense from anyone. He knew he presented an intimidating figure. He knew he had a reputation as a tough guy . . . and he was quite happy to keep it that way. Smith, for all that, was very similar to Peter Storey in that he never complained about being kicked himself. Often, immediately after a game, I have seen Storey's shins bruised and bleeding.

Bremner and Giles were not alone in being hard men in Revie's Leeds. Norman Hunter would kick you as soon as look at you. Yet off the field he was as kind and as nice a man as you could ever meet. Leeds, as a team, could look after themselves. They could play the game any way you wanted. If you felt like trying to match them for skill, they would take you on. If you wanted to mix it, they would fight you.

Pat Jennings says the only booking he got through his entire career was against Leeds. Leeds would stand on the goal-keeper as he tried to clear the ball. Pat was with Tottenham at the time, and Mick Jones whacked him as he went to clear. Pat, and it was rare for him, lost his temper and kicked out at Jones. The referee saw it and booked him.

We once played at Elland Road after Sammy Nelson had broken his nose in training earlier in the week. The game had only been going a few minutes when Sammy got a knock on it. He needed treatment and Leeds realised he was playing with a broken nose. The elbows were flying in after that. They were actually chasing his broken nose.

A Leeds player of that era for whom I had no time at all was Allan Clarke. He would come in late at you. I saw him catch Liam Brady at Highbury one day with a particularly nasty challenge. Liam went mad. If he had not been restrained I think he would have done Clarke a serious injury. I rated Clarke a superb finisher. But he always seemed very dour. That was the way he struck me, anyway.

One of the toughest centre-forwards I have come across was Joe Jordan. He was very good in the air, had pace, and was a strong runner. When corners came over, you always knew there was a good chance of both you and the ball ending up in the net. Joe always regarded goalkeepers as legitimate targets. For all that, he was as brave as they come. He used to take his false teeth out before a game. At the kick-off he would give you his famous snarl. I have known experienced pros to be frightened by it, never mind youngsters.

I had heard that he was a heck of a nice man off the field. But it was just something I couldn't believe. Then Joy and I were on holiday in Florida one year, when Joe turned up with his family. They were great company and I came home thinking how misguided folks were about Joe. I played against him the next season and the game had only been going a couple of minutes when he whacked me. It was as if we had never met! For all that, I admire him tremendously and we have stayed good friends over the years.

My first meeting with Peter Withe was when he was with Birmingham City. He smashed me across the ear. I went down in considerable pain and it was Peter who helped me up, saying, "Sorry son. Are you OK?" I thought at first, what a nice lad. But it kept happening. It was Peter who taught me that players will take advantage of you if you can't and won't look after yourself.

My first encounter with Graeme Souness was when he was at Middlesbrough. He oozed class. He never had real pace, but he read situations brilliantly and was always able to make time and space for himself.

He had just been signed by Liverpool when we met them that time in the Milk Cup semi-final. He came into the players' lounge after the match at Anfield and looked a lost soul. It was being said then that he was too much of a troublemaker to be a Liverpool player. He proved all his critics wrong.

Years later, we played Liverpool in the Milk Cup at Highbury. There was a bit of trouble between Ray Kennedy and Arsenal's Peter Nicholas. In the return game at Anfield, after about ten minutes, Graeme clinically and coldly went for Nicholas. They took poor Peter off on a stretcher for his leg to be stitched. The players knew what had happened, but the referee didn't spot it. The incident was no surprise to Nicholas. He was expecting it.

Personally, I always got on well with Souness. For me, he was not unlike Johnny Giles in that his mean streak was allied to a level of ability you could only admire. It is strange, though, how things work out. At Anfield, the police always stand near the dressing-room door. In Graeme's early days with the club, one of them came in after we had played there and said, "He won't last long here. He's a thug." How wrong can you be?

Yes, I liked Souness. I still do. But I know Liam Brady wasn't keen on him at all. Whenever Arsenal played Liverpool, they always seemed to have words. You could sense a certain tension between them. Graeme was never going to win many nice guy awards. But, at his peak, I think most of us would have liked him on our side.

One of the best centre-forwards I ever played against was Martin Chivers, when he was at Tottenham. But a hard edge was the one thing Martin lacked. He was a gentle giant. For a big man, he had wonderful balance and his shooting was ferocious. But he didn't like the physical side of the game.

Among the current crop of centre-forwards, Mick Harford is as hard as they come. He is in the Joe Jordan mould and it is a fact that central defenders don't look forward to their encounters with Mick. He has come up the hard way, serving his apprenticeship in the lower divisions. I think he is a better player for that sort of soccer upbringing.

He was a Birmingham City player when I first came up against him. He gave me a tough game then and nothing since has changed. I have always enjoyed my battles with Harford, but if we have played Luton in recent years and he has not been in the side I have not been exactly displeased. It is a lot easier when he is not around.

Some centre-forwards can go a whole match without saying a word to you. With Mick, despite the toughness of the battle, there is always something said between us. We played at Luton in Don Howe's last season as Arsenal's manager and I ran to meet a long kick from their keeper. I went to make contact with the ball, and Mick caught me. I had to go off and I thought I had broken my jaw.

Viv Anderson was going away on an England trip at the time, and he said to Luton's Ricky Hill, "Tell Mick Harford to watch it next time we play you. David O'Leary is looking for him." Actually, I hadn't said any such thing. Viv was just getting Ricky at it.

Later that season we played Luton in a Cup game. Mick and I could almost have been old friends, it went so smoothly. It was a smashing battle. One we both enjoyed. There has never ever been a hint of trouble between us since.

I know, if there is one centre-forward I would always like to have in my side, it is Mick Harford. He is totally unselfish. His contribution to the team stretches over the whole 90 minutes. He gets back and defends at set pieces as well as any centre-forward I have played against. His partnership with Brian Stein was one of the best around, and I believe Harford is desperately unlucky to have received such scant recognition at international level.

For a couple of years, Paul Mariner ranked alongside the best I have ever seen. I was at Lilleshall for special training with the Republic of Ireland squad at the time Johnny Giles tried to sign Mariner for West Bromwich. Bobby Robson, then the Ipswich manager, got in first and took Paul to Portman Road. Giles was very disappointed and told the Irish lads, "Robson has got a real gem there."

Paul had a lovely touch for a big man. He was excellent in the air, and when the going got tough he could dish it out with the best of them. You could never afford to relax against him. He was alert to the slightest lapse in a defender's concentration.

Mariner was still a good player when he came to Arsenal, but there was little doubt in my mind that his best days had been spent at Ipswich. But Don Howe knew I was a Mariner admirer and the England connection had given him first-hand knowledge of Paul's qualities.

Just how good John Fashanu will be is something for the future. His potential is enormous. He is strong and he has good pace. He also has an intimidating physical presence. He is definitely tougher and better than his brother Justin.

Justin was an out-and-out target man. I always felt a highly promising career started to go backwards when he got the label of a million pounds man after Brian Clough signed him for Nottingham Forest. It wasn't his fault, but he found it almost impossible to live up to what was expected of him after that. His strength was in the air, but Forest played to feet. That didn't help.

For me, John is already the better of the two brothers. He is always talking to you during a game. Any time you are involved in a free kick with John he will say, "You coming in to mix it with me?" It is a challenge I usually find hard to resist. He isn't dirty. You have a go at him, he will have a go back. That's fair enough.

In the ranking list of strikers I have come up against in the First Division over the years, Ian Rush is the best. His pace is a killer. Luckily, I was blessed with a bit of pace myself. Believe me, you need to be in fifth gear all the time to stay with him. Ian is always at your shoulder, waiting to get in behind you.

He is a lethal finisher . . . the best I have ever seen. Playing against him is a real challenge. He is not hard. It is more a battle of pace and wits. Off the pitch and away from the action I have to say I don't know Rush at all. He never talks during a game and he has always struck me as a rather quiet lad – not at all big-headed.

What makes Rush particularly hard to play against is that he never stands still. Central defenders like strikers to stand in front of them . . . where you can see them. Rush 'loses' defenders because of his movement.

Gary Lineker is very similar to Rush. Like the Welsh ace, he relies on blistering pace. I would have loved to see him come to Arsenal when he left Leicester. At one time it seemed a possibility, but he went to Everton. He is not that dangerous when the ball is played to his feet. He is at his best when it is put behind defenders. He always seems a very confident lad. Very chirpy – and very different to Rush.

Strikers usually hunt in pairs. In that context, during my time, Rush and Kenny Dalglish have been the very best. Dalglish, I would have to say, is the best all-round footballer to have played in the First Division in my time. I found him a bit of a moaner, but his work-rate was phenomenal, and he was a winner. He had this acute awareness. He could see a situation in a split second and take advantage of it. While he wouldn't knock his own players, he still demanded perfection from those around him.

The prefix "great" is applied to so many players. In Kenny's case, however, it truly fits. He isn't tall, but he would lean into the biggest of centre-halves to stop them getting power into their headers. For a couple of seasons with Liverpool I rated him the best player in the world. If he had been playing for an Italian or West German team I have no doubt he would have been voted European Footballer of the Year more than once. I know I voted for him as the PFA Player of the Year several times. His partnership with Rush was surely one of the most formidable of all time in this country.

Now Liverpool have Peter Beardsley. He is not as good as Dalglish . . . but who is? I still think he is world-class. I first met Peter when he was playing for Vancouver Whitecaps with my brother Pierce. I came back to Arsenal and recommended him strongly. The club looked at him. But the feedback I got at the time was that he was a good astroturf player. Off the field, Peter is one of the most modest players I have ever met. He is totally uncomplicated. When he was in Canada, Peter was offered the chance to play for them in the World Cup if he took out Canadian citizenship. What a loss that would have been for England!

Graeme Sharp is a hit-man who never seems to have captured the public's imagination. Yet people in the game know how good he is. He is so resilient. He is top-class at holding the ball up and bringing his midfield men into the game.

I am also a fan of Andy Gray. He is anything but a big man, yet he is one of the best headers of a ball I have come across. He is also brave . . . possibly too brave for his own good. Andy has one of the biggest hearts football has ever seen. He was always diving in among the flying boots. That is why he got so many injuries. I also found Andy to be one of the game's moaners and groaners. Half the time, however, I couldn't understand what he was saying!

As an out-and-out goal-getter, Malcolm Macdonald was one of the best. He was certainly the best scoring striker Arsenal had for many years. He would collect 20 goals in a bad season. He loved scoring goals – and claiming them too! A shot would hit three defenders on the way in, but Malcolm would still say it was his goal. I once remember Frank Stapleton getting above Brian Greenhoff to power a tremendous header towards the net at Highbury. The ball was going over the line when Malcolm volleyed it. He insisted it was his goal. He was obsessed with scoring, and for a striker that is no bad thing.

You would always see Malcolm with books under his arm. Usually, they were books of great social significance. We never saw him actually reading any of them. Malcolm loved the spotlight. For all that, he was a hard man and he always wanted to be a winner. I liked him . . . I really did. Alan Ball always reckoned Malcolm couldn't trap a bag of cement, while agreeing he was a scorer supreme. But Malcolm had his golden years, and nobody can take that away from him.

I first played against Garry Thompson when he was up front with Mark Hateley at Coventry. At that time I would have backed him to go all the way. He was outstanding in the air. Yet somehow he never seems to have made the most of all that potential.

Getting above Everton's Graeme Sharp in a match at Highbury.

I think about the top hit men of my time, and any list would be incomplete without Kevin Keegan. I always felt Kenny Dalglish lost him on ability. But Kevin had this incredible inner strength . . . a deep-seated determination to overcome his deficiencies in order to be the best. Keegan was at his peak, I felt, when he went to play for Hamburg in West Germany and was voted European Footballer of the Year.

Liverpool generally have not gone in for big target men over the years. But that is what John Toshack was. He was outstanding in the air. I was 17 when I first played against him. Little Kevin knew instinctively where all Tosh's flicks were going. It was uncanny. As a pairing, I still thought Rush and Dalglish were better, though.

Now Liverpool have John Aldridge, John Barnes and Peter Beardsley . . . a trio who made life hell for First Division defenders last season. It couldn't have been easy for Barnes, going into the cauldron that is Anfield. Yet there wasn't a more exciting player in the whole country. I feel he is at his most effective when he is floating . . . getting the ball and going at defenders. He can hold it up as well as anybody, too, before playing people in. Played wide, Barnes can also be devastatingly effective. He has a great fitness level and is exceptionally strong.

I don't need to state a case for Aldridge. His scoring record at all his clubs does that. When Rush departed for Juventus, Aldridge was the best available marksman in this country. That is why Liverpool bought him.

CHAPTER SEVENTEEN

Graham – Best Yet

George Graham is the first manager for whom I have signed a contract before the old one expired. There were no protracted negotiations, no disputes, no second thoughts. Just straight-forward talking on both sides and an all-round willingness to put Arsenal first and get on with the job. That tells you everything about how I see the man who is now manager of the club that has dominated my adult life.

Mr Graham had been at Arsenal no more than a week when Steve Burtenshaw, who had been caretaker-manager following Don Howe's departure, telephoned me to say, "The new boss wants to see you at 11 o'clock the day after tomorrow."

I arrived at Highbury, and Theo Foley, who had come from Millwall with George Graham to be his assistant at Highbury, was in the corridor. I had got to know him over the years from his days as Charlton manager, from meeting him at various functions, and because of his Irish connections. Theo has always been the same to me – a bubbly, full-of-life character who smiles easily and gets uptight very rarely. I can only remember him ever once being in a bad mood during the time he has been at Arsenal.

What happens usually on a training morning is that Theo

comes out at 10.15 to do the warm-up. The boss will join us 15 minutes later to take the session. This particular morning, Theo didn't get us out on time. It was raining hard and the manager wasn't pleased. That put Theo in a bad mood. He had a black look all morning and made the players suffer by sending us on punishment runs.

After exchanging a couple of pleasantries with Theo that morning of my first meeting with the man the directors had chosen to replace Don Howe, I knocked on the manager's door and went in. I said to him, "I presume it will be 'Boss?'"

He answered,

"Absolutely correct. It will be 'Boss' or 'Mr Graham.'"

My contract was up and he had obviously done his homework. The impression I got was that he was classing everyone the same. We were all starting fresh, with anything and everything that had happened in the past now a part of the club's history. I was being offered a one-year contract. There was no room for negotiation. I had the feeling that if I didn't like it I could go. We were now in May. I had a testimonial scheduled for 5 August. I wasn't going to sign anything until I got my game. I wondered at that time whether the boss really appreciated the depth of feeling I had for Arsenal. I came home musing to myself just how much Mr Graham knew of what had been going on at the club.

That first meeting ended with my saying I would think about the one-year deal that had been offered. What worried me was that people might think I wanted to have my game, stay for a year, then run.

Two weeks later I got a call from Mr Graham. He wanted to come and see me at my home. I said to him, "You will be more than welcome." He came round and I was deeply impressed as he detailed his plans for Arsenal and explained his methods of management. I realised that here was a manager who knew what he wanted and knew exactly what he was doing.

I like to think he knows me well enough now to appreciate my own ambitions . . . the one that tops all others being to win a First Division championship medal with Arsenal.

It's up there somewhere! A League game against Chelsea.

After that meeting at my home, we both knew where we stood. I signed the one-year deal that had been offered just three weeks before my testimonial. The boss was very fair. He said he was assessing the situation with all the players, it wouldn't take him long . . . and we would all know where we stood. The incentive was there for me – as it was for every player of the club. I just didn't want it to be a wasted season, with another drawn-out series of talks in a year's time.

When we all reported for pre-season training, there was a feeling of apprehension throughout the club. It was understandable. This was a new regime and nobody really knew what to expect.

The boss got us all together. Without holding a gun to anyone's head, he laid down the law. He said he would treat us like men, but discipline would be tight. He didn't expect us to behave like saints . . . but he made it clear he was concerned about some of the bad publicity the club had been getting off the field. There was no room for doubt on that score . . . things had to change.

Our new manager said that whether we found him a good boss to work for or a bad one would be up to us. He didn't bully, there was no suggestion he intended to rule by fear. But the guidelines had been set.

We started our preparations for the new season with an eight-day trip to Ireland. In many ways, it was a voyage of discovery. There wasn't any uncertainty or wavering among the players . . . this was a manager we could respect.

Personally – and it was a view that was shared – I found his training excellent. Don Howe – and I wouldn't want it thought I didn't have the greatest respect for him – used to put a lot of emphasis on physical work. He would say, "If Seb Coe can do it, so can you." Under Mr Graham the most running we ever do is shuttle work over 30 yards. Pre-season, Don was a great one for weight training, cross-country and lapping the pitch. With the boss, we've not done much cross-country, but we've gone in for a lot of sprint work. Certainly, I have not felt any less fit. In fact, at the end of the season, I have felt fresher than I did with Don.

When Viv Anderson joined Arsenal from Nottingham Forest he said he thought he had joined a running club . . . not a football club. I get the impression George Graham has learned and benefited from all the people he has played and worked for, notably Bertie Mee, Dave Sexton, Don and Terry Venables. I can see the best of all of them in the boss.

Isn't that the art of good management? Taking the best and discarding the rest. Mr Graham's organisation is first-class. He makes the training interesting, makes sure the season doesn't start to drag. It makes coming into work a pleasure. He wants players to be resilient, to be tough. But won't tolerate anyone going over the top. His principles on that point have my total support.

The boss works particularly hard on perfecting our defensive system. I think in season 1986-87 Arsenal's back four of Anderson, Tony Adams, myself and Kenny Sansom was as good as any defensive unit I have played in.

We've won the Cup! Saluting Arsenal's fans at Wembley after beating Liverpool in the 1987 Littlewoods Cup Final at Wembley.

We played Sporting Lisbon in our first pre-season game when the new management team took over. What the boss had to say at half-time deeply impressed me. He analysed all our performances individually, picked out points he particularly wanted to emphasise and made the maximum use of the few minutes a manager has at half-time to put things right. I knew then we were going into the new season with the right man at the top.

For the first time in my years at Highbury, we were about to employ a defensive system where the two centre-backs would run the offsides . . . where Tony Adams and I would dictate when to push up and when to stay put. It was a pleasure to be in the back four. It was a bit like joining a new club – without leaving the comforts and familiarity of the old one.

George Graham's greatest triumph in that first year, of course, was to win the Littlewoods Cup. He had been taken on to put Arsenal back on the map. Nobody could deny that coming from behind to beat Liverpool the way we did at Wembley was a great start.

While he has learned from others, it is beyond argument that George Graham is also very much his own man . . . innovating ideas and doing the job with style. Training under Don brought too much pressure at times. It was so intensified, it got to some of the younger players. There was enough pressure in playing twice a week. You don't see that now – though we work just as hard. The boss and Theo are very much a team. Theo has a great *rapport* with the players and acts as a sort of buffer between us and the manager.

If the spirit in a football club is right, with everyone working together, it comes through when you are up against it. The fact that we had now got it right at Arsenal came through for me in our epic semi-final struggle against Tottenham when we won the Littlewoods Cup. We were 1-0 down from the first leg and it was not a healthy position as we faced the return. We travelled across North London to White Hart Lane and the boss said, "We don't have to win the tie here . . . only the game." The point was pushed home that a 1-0 victory would take us into a third match and provide a fresh platform for reaching Wembley.

But Clive Allen scored for Spurs after 20 minutes and we went in at the interval 2-0 down on aggregate. It looked a pretty hopeless position and the heads were well and truly down as we walked into the dressing-room. A lot of us were wondering whether Viv Anderson would be pushed up to centre-forward to lead us into a sort of Custer's last stand. What the boss had to say was inspirational. Part of what he said was, "We'll keep our heads. We won't panic. We will continue to create chances . . . only we will put them away this half."

What he did was settle us all down. He was under pressure himself – but it didn't show. Viv Anderson and Niall Quinn scored, we pulled back to 2-2 and earned ourselves a third crack. We lost the toss for choice of grounds and had to go back to White Hart Lane. But nothing would stop us now. We won 2-1 and we were at Wembley.

Spirit? Wembley proved just how far we had come in that direction. Ian Rush gave Liverpool the lead and the thought that Liverpool don't lose when he scores first for them went through a lot of minds. We buried that hoodoo. Our 2-1 win was one of the best performances in all my years at the club.

In January of that season the boss came to me one day when we were training at Highbury. The session was over and I was in the bath. He asked if I would come to see him in his office. He came straight to the point. He wanted me to sign a new long-term contract. We got together a week later and a few days after that I committed myself to Arsenal for a further four years.

When it came to contract discussions, he was the most positive manager I have ever dealt with. If he had been in charge at Highbury at the time Liam Brady and then Frank Stapleton went, it is possible they would still be Arsenal players. I put my name to a new deal six months before the old agreement was due to expire. I was delighted.

The boss was getting flak from the media at the time over contracts that were about to end and had not been renegotiated. He could have got a lot of mileage in the Press over agreeing a fresh deal with me, yet he wanted it kept quiet.

When season 1987-88 started, I had three years to go on that contract. There is no way my ambitions for Arsenal are any less than when I first came to Highbury 15 years ago. I want to see this contract out, earn another one and play on for a further two years. I think the next five years could be great ones for Arsenal . . . and I very much want to remain part of the scene. I want to finish as a 20-year, one-club man.

George Graham is a manager who keeps his distance from the players. I believe that is the way it should be. At the same time he has made it clear he will always be available if you have a problem and need to see him.

We have always worn collar-and-tie for away games and when officially representing the club. The boss has taken it a stage further, insisting on club blazer and flannels for away matches and in all appearances in public on club business. He has made it clear how important it is to be good ambassadors off the field as well as on it.

While discipline is tight under Mr Graham, I would have to say the atmosphere is more relaxed. It was only in his last year at Arsenal that Don let the tension fall away in training. It added so much to the enjoyment we got out of playing the game.

At the time George Graham got the job, the media were making Terry Venables and Graham Taylor the front-runners. At one stage I have little doubt they were. But I have no doubt now that the board made the right choice. The boss is an Arsenal man through and through. I don't think he ever lost his love for the club that gave him his greatest days as a player. Even when he was manager of Millwall he lived in North London, not that far from Highbury. I believe he now has the best club job in football – with the best club chairman.

Perhaps one day, George Graham would make the perfect manager for Scotland. But Arsenal would miss him, and I also think he would miss the day-to-day involvement you get with club football.

CHAPTER EIGHTEEN

The Injury Fear Factor

Serious injury is something all players dread. Serious injury in an Eastern European country, where the medical treatment can often be primitive, is the professional footballer's nightmare.

I am a fatalist about these things. I take the view that what will be, will be. If you look at it any other way, you will never be able to do your job properly. It is like a butcher who cuts his finger. Getting injured is an occupational hazard.

What we all fear most, I suppose, is a badly broken leg. One of the worst tackles I ever saw was responsible for one of the worst injuries I have witnessed. It happened in Sofia, where the Republic of Ireland were playing Bulgaria. It made me realise that if you are going to get injured, you must hope it doesn't happen in a place like Sofia.

Jimmy Holmes went for a 50-50 ball just inside our half. This big Bulgarian came right over the top and broke Jimmy's leg. Johnny Giles went over to him and gently rolled down his sock. The bone was pushing through the skin. It was awful. I saw Jimmy grip Gilesy's hand to stop himself screaming with the pain. He was carried off and taken to hospital in Sofia. Once he went into the care of the Bulgarians, our own medical man, the very capable Dr Bob O'Driscoll, had to surrender all authority. We were all very subdued when we got back to our hotel.

We were due to fly home the following morning and we were concerned about what would happen to Jimmy. The Bulgarians had tried to reset the shattered bone under a local anaesthetic. Doc O'Driscoll was fuming. Jimmy begged the doctor to take him back with us. After careful thought, it was agreed it would be preferable to risk moving him rather than leave him to the Bulgarians. They had not made an impressive start.

Jimmy was brought to our Swissair flight in an ambulance and made as comfortable as possible in the first-class section. But he was in agony. As soon as the plane landed in Geneva, Jimmy was taken off and rushed to a Swiss clinic. The Swiss doctors, we heard later, were furious at the poor job that had been done in Sofia. They couldn't believe the state the leg was in and the way Jimmy had been treated. He stayed in the Swiss clinic for a week before being transferred to a hospital in North London. I went to see him there. The treatment in Bulgaria had been so poor that the leg had turned septic. He was still in pain when I saw him.

Jimmy never recovered to play at the highest level again. His days as an international player were over. The next time I saw him he had left Tottenham and was playing in Canada for the Vancouver Whitecaps. It was good just to see him playing again.

Luck, however, continued to elude Jimmy. The Republic arranged a testimonial in Dublin for him – against Tottenham. But the Heysel Stadium tragedy happened and English clubs were banned from playing abroad. A frantic rescue operation got under way and an all-star team was put together to play for Jimmy. I remember travelling over to Dublin with Chris Waddle, Ossie Ardiles, Pat Jennings and Steve Wicks. The Tottenham chairman Irving Scholar was also on the flight. For a game put together so quickly Jimmy got a good gate – 15,000. It was no less than he deserved.

Muscle strain is the injury all professional footballers learn to live with. Strains to the groin, thigh and calf are bound to happen when you play so many matches over such a concentrated period of time. Most of us play when we are not one hundred per cent fit. Once the season gets under way, there isn't much alternative. It is often a question of rest, play, then rest again.

These days, with small, tight squads, clubs cannot afford to wait for a player to say he is totally free of aches and pains. When you are a key player it doesn't even matter how big the club's squad is. You are only earning your money when you are out there playing.

It was trying to play on when I knew deep down it was wrong that brought me my biggest disappointment in the game. We were playing Nottingham Forest at Highbury on Boxing Day 1987 when I got injured. Nigel Clough and I sprinted for a ball that had been hit down the line by Forest left-back Graham Pearce. Young Nigel suddenly pulled up quickly. He knew that his hamstring had gone. He went off right away and was out of the game for nearly two months.

All the tension of a Spurs–Arsenal derby as I clash with Paul Miller.

It was one of those awful, hard-to-explain ironies – but at exactly the same moment I felt a sensation in my Achilles' tendon. It stretched and then seemed to settle back. But I knew it wasn't right. I went in at half-time and it was agreed with manager George Graham and physiotherapist Gary Lewin that I should come off.

At that time, the club didn't think there was anything seriously wrong. But, typical of Arsenal's thoroughness, they wanted another opinion. I was sent to see Paul Aichroth, a leader in the sports injuries field, at Wellington Clinic in London's St John's Wood. It was his opinion that three weeks of complete rest would see me OK again. I only went to see him after playing against Millwall in the third round of the FA Cup. I had to tell him I had played with the injury since first doing it against Forest. He was very surprised, saying, "Achilles' tendon trouble is not something you can run off. Play on, and the condition can become chronic."

I was examined by Mr Aichroth five days after playing against Millwall. On the next Saturday we were away to Liverpool. I was rested from this one because Arsenal wanted to give me every chance of playing against Sheffield Wednesday in the quarter-finals of the Littlewoods Cup at Hillsborough the following Wednesday. I played at Wednesday, but only with increasing discomfort. We won 1-0, though, and at the time that seemed to make it all worthwhile. I'm not blaming anyone other than myself. The bottom line is that I wanted to play, even though I knew I was not doing myself any good.

Before we travelled to Sheffield, I told Mr Aichroth I was playing. He thought it was a mistake but I know he understood and accepted why I was willing to take the risk. I knew I was taking a chance. I also realised I was jeopardising my chance of an international recall. But I was trapped . . . by the success Arsenal were enjoying and by the smallness of the club's first-team squad.

We played Manchester United the following Sunday in a live television game. I played, we lost 2-1, and I was left wondering whether it was worth it. The tendon was getting more and more sore. I didn't train at all between the Wednesday and United matches.

I started to train again, if you could call it that, on the Wednesday after the United game. I did a couple of laps of the Highbury pitch on the Thursday and Friday and played in the FA Cup at Brighton on Saturday. It was a very heavy pitch, and that didn't help.

I was just about getting through the games. We won 2-1 down on the Sussex coast, and for me personally it had been a struggle. We were keeping my injury under wraps. Nobody, with the exception of my wife Joy, knew just how bad it was.

We went to Marbella to prepare for Everton in the semi-finals of the Littlewoods Cup. I travelled with the squad. It was important for the spirit of togetherness the boss had built up. But while the others trained hard, all I managed was a couple of short runs. Most of my time was spent getting treatment from Gary Lewin.

I managed to play in the first leg at Goodison Park, where we beat Everton 1-0. I got through that one, too. But the matches were becoming more and more of an ordeal. I was now getting out of bed in the mornings like an old man, treading very gingerly and needing to do stretching excercises before I could get any real movement. Even worse, I was beginning to walk with a pronounced limp.

We played Luton in the League at Highbury – it was the day Lee Dixon, signed by the boss from Stoke, made his debut. That was the game that convinced me the tendon was now in a bad way. The Luton players knew I was struggling. My old adversary Mick Harford asked, "Which leg do I need to kick?" – adding sympathetically, "You ought to go off."

In the week that followed, I did the minimum of training. We were playing Manchester United in the fifth round of the FA Cup that coming Saturday – another vital match in a whole series of them. Gary did a great job trying to settle the tendon down so that I would be able to get through the 90 minutes. Virtually my only training now was on an exercise bike.

I played against Manchester United. But I knew after only a few minutes that I would never last out the game. I finally came off 15 minutes from the end. We were leading 2-1 and it stayed that way.

The crunch was to come the following Wednesday when we faced Everton in the second leg of the Littlewoods Cup semi-final at Highbury. I desperately wanted to play. I think the club were keen to get me out there too. The plan, in fact, was for me to try to last it out for 60 minutes. We believed Everton would throw everything at us in that time and endeavour to put us under heavy pressure. It was felt that if we weathered the storm we would be on our way to Wembley.

We beat them comfortably. I managed to stay on for 70 minutes before limping off. The leg now was in an awful state.

The next big hurdle was the FA Cup quarter-final with Nottingham Forest at Highbury. First Division games against Charlton and Tottenham came first and the aim was to sit out those matches and get patched up again for the next Cup clash. I started the Forest tie. But it was no good. I realised that straight from the kick-off. I came off after 25 minutes. The score at that time was 0-0. My spirits were at rock-bottom.

I didn't mess about. I went straight into the bath. I was there when the other players came in at half-time. Whatever happened in the FA Cup, I knew then, deep down, that I was going to miss the Littlewoods Cup final. I was still sunk deep in the bath when Tony Donnelly, our kit manager, came in and said Forest had gone in front through Paul Wilkinson. Forest went on to win 2-1. Our dream of getting to two Cup finals was shattered. It had been a bad day.

I saw Gary Lewin and the club doctors John Crane and Leonard Sash the Monday after we went out to Forest. It was agreed I should be examined again by Paul Aichroth. It was the following Monday when I went to see him. Later, Gary said to me, "There are six weeks to go before Wembley. We want you to rest for a month." We were scheduled to play Watford nine days before the Littlewoods Cup final. It was planned for me to use that League match as a testing ground for Wembley.

No time for smiles on match day.

Mr Aichroth was in agreement and was hopeful a month's rest might just get me through the two games. Gary got hold of a couple of racing bikes and for three weeks we did 15 miles a day on the roads around the training ground. Now it wasn't only my Achilles' tendon that was sore! We used to do our biking in the mornings. I spent the afternoons on the treatment table.

Two days into the week of the Watford game, I knew my leg still wasn't right. For all Gary's dedication and hard work there had been no noticeable improvement. On the Tuesday I played in my first reserve team match for 13 years. I had no basic fitness problem but then I was not really extended. All that match proved to me was how much the standard of reserve team football has deteriorated over the years. I trained for half-an-hour on Thursday and accepted the time had arrived for me to concede defeat.

I talked with Gary and he arranged for me to see John Crane, the Arsenal doctor who is also the England doctor, that afternoon. Doc Crane agreed I wouldn't make Wembley. I felt as sorry for Gary Lewin as I did for myself. He had worked so hard trying to get me right. I drove home, with Gary saying the club would try to get me into hospital right away for an operation.

All I wanted now was to have the operation and bring down the curtain on a season that, for so long, had promised so much. But Mr Aichroth was away and I had to wait until the Wednesday before Wembley before anything could be done.

I didn't go to the Watford game. I didn't feel in the mood to have to stand answering questions about why I wasn't playing and did I still hope to make the final. The rest of the squad went off to Marbella to prepare for the Wembley meeting with Luton . . . and I got ready to go into hospital.

The great thing about a club like Arsenal is that you know, if you are unlucky enough to get a bad injury, the treatment will be the best. I went into the Wellington Hospital on the Wednesday morning and was operated on later that day. I had torn the tendon fibres and they had to be trimmed off. It wasn't a case of saving David O'Leary's career. Serious enough, but with no complications. I was grateful for that. Mr Aichroth had shaken my hand as I was wheeled into the operating theatre and said, "Sorry it had to come to this." But the operation was a success, and that was what mattered.

I woke up in my private room and the attention was fantastic. It was typical of the way Arsenal look after their players. The most difficult decision I had to make in hospital was what to have for lunch. The only disappointment was watching on television from my hospital bed as Luton brought off a shock win.

That Sunday morning the newspapers were full of predictions, colour pieces and stories about the final. Not being part of it left me very depressed. I got a telephone call from Ken Friar, Arsenal's secretary and managing director, just before the game. He knew I would be feeling pretty low, and he said: "Don't feel too down. There will be other finals after this one." I appreciated that call.

But what had started as a tendon strain had ended with one of the biggest disappointments of my career. It happens in football and I have been in the game long enough not to let it fester inside me. I knew it was important to try to play.

It was around that time that Liverpool's Mark Lawrenson had been forced to quit as a player by a tendon injury. I think, for a while, people were trying to compare every tendon injury with the one that forced Mark to give up playing. But Mark's tendon had snapped – and that is rare. Glenn Hoddle, Mick Harford, Paul Mariner, Kevin Sheedy, Graham Rix, Peter Reid and Paul McGrath are among players who have needed tendon operations and come back to play as well as ever.

One thing about getting injured as a professional footballer is that our union, the Professional Footballers' Association, has helped make sure players at every level get the best possible treatment. Perhaps, in the past, players at clubs such as Arsenal, Manchester United and Liverpool have been spoiled. Now, because of the good work done by the PFA, it is nice to know that you can be with a Third or Fourth Division side and get just the same treatment.

It was the first time I had missed a really important match

because of injury. It made me appreciate the finals I had actually played in all the more. And I couldn't help thinking about Tottenham's Danny Thomas. His career had been cut short before even reaching its prime, by a tackle from a Queen's Park Rangers player. I felt for Danny, a lad who was liked and respected by everyone in the game. If something similar ever happened to me I would drag whoever was responsible through the courts. There are crude tackles, intentionally dirty tackles, and those who are responsible for them should not be allowed to get away with it. Tackles that maim are not something we can sweep into a dark corner as if they didn't happen. There will always be mistimed tackles and bad injuries, but we are all professionals and we all know the damage an irresponsible challenge can do.

I have been lucky with the physiotherapists at Arsenal. Fred Street, who did the job when I came to the club, was superb. England are lucky and privileged to have him. Clubs can release valuable players to go on England international duty knowing their physical welfare will be looked after by the very best in Fred and Doctor John Crane.

Gary Lewin, who is Arsenal's current physiotherapist, used to be a goalkeeper at the club. He reached 18, a decision had to be made about becoming a full professional, and Gary realised he wasn't good enough to make it to the top. It was Fred who suggested he study to be a physio. That way he could keep an interest in the game. Gary went to work at Guy's Hospital, passed all his examinations, and came back to Highbury to work part-time. Now he is the number one. He loves the job and the club. All the players call him 'Bloodthirsty Lew' because he likes to watch whenever a player has an operation. But we all like him. The players know Gary will work 24-hours-a-day if there is a chance to get one of us right for a big game.

Gary isn't the only young player indebted to Fred. Derek Wright was an apprentice professional at Arsenal around the time I got into the first team. He was a hard, rugged full-back or central defender . . . a Newcastle United fanatic. But he didn't make it. Fred encouraged him to take up physiotherapy. Like Gary, he passed his exams. Derek got a job on the medical staff at Fulham and is now first-team physio at his beloved Newcastle.

They don't come any more fanatical than Derek. At Highbury, for first-team games, the apprentices used to sit in the paddock area behind the dug-out. Once, when we played Newcastle, he sat there wearing a Newcastle scarf and bobble hat . . . screaming his head off for the Geordies. And he was an Arsenal player!

CHAPTER NINETEEN

Partners

Central defenders have one thing in common with strikers. They go in pairs. The best complement one another. It is their strength.

In Arsenal's double year, Frank McLintock and Peter Simpson were a team within a team when it came to repelling raiders. They knew what the other was going to do almost before he did it. Their understanding was close to being telepathic. I had the same comfortable feeling such togetherness brings when playing alongside Mark Lawrenson for the Republic of Ireland . . . with Willie Young during four great years at Arsenal, and in the short time I have partnered Tony Adams.

Willie Young, for me, presents the perfect example of a central defender who was never going to be the greatest on his own, but put together with someone who would blend in with his strengths, could do an outstanding job.

More than anything, Willie wanted to be a winner. But alongside him, it was essential to have someone who was mobile. Whenever the opposition pumped the ball our way, Willie wanted to go and attack it. That was OK, because I would take care of whoever was dropping off around him.

Over a period, I thought we made up an excellent partnership. There were some bad moments and some matches when it went wrong. But playing alongside Willie was generally a genuine pleasure.

My first central defensive partner in the First Division was Terry Mancini. That was nearly 14 years ago. I have rarely come across a player with a better attitude. 'Henry's' ability might have been limited but the size of his heart was unbelievable.

He didn't have a lot of pace and strikers who were a bit quick troubled him. But during my uncertain early days as an Arsenal first-team player he helped me enormously. I still remember vividly the first game we played as a partnership . . . at Burnley. He talked me through it after patiently providing a run-down of the strengths and weaknesses of every Burnley player.

That season, there was no regular pairing at the heart of Arsenal's defence. Usually, it was me, with Terry Mancini or Peter Simpson as a partner. Peter, or 'Stan' as we all knew him, was at the veteran stage. If you could have injected 'Stan's' ability into 'Henry' or Mancini's attitude into Simpson, you would have had the best central defender in the country.

Simpson should have been an England regular. He was a smashing fellow who wouldn't do an ounce of harm to anyone. But he was so laid back. It was often said at Highbury that lack of real ambition cost 'Stan' England caps.

Mancini would bubble before a game. His enthusiasm was infectious. 'Stan' would sit beside you in the dressing-room and say things like, "Don't know if my knee will stand up to it" . . . "We shouldn't be playing football in this weather" . . . "The pitch will be too heavy for me" . . . "I don't really fancy it today." He hated to have to make decisions. Buying a new car, for instance, was something that would have him in a quandary for weeks. What colour should he go for? . . . should he have a sun roof?

But everyone liked 'Stan'. His best friend was little George Armstrong. They were inseparable. Yet they were complete opposites. George was always on the go. He never stopped wanting to do things. He would come home from a 20-mile training run and start to paint the house. 'Stan' would get home and want to have a sleep.

As Simpson faded from the Highbury scene in the 1976-77 season, Pat Howard arrived from Newcastle. Pat was a good, honest player. He wanted to win the ball and was happy if people were covering around him. He was not unlike Terry Mancini, but he didn't have the same bubbly personality.

Really, it was a season of change. With a couple of months left, Willie Young arrived from Tottenham. I knew he had been bought to play alongside me. Terry Neill knew him from when they were together at White Hart Lane and was convinced Willie could do a good job for Arsenal. He wasn't wrong.

We played together for the first time in April against Leicester at Highbury. It was the day Graham Rix made his debut. I scored twice, Graham got a goal, we won 3-0, and Willie and I hit it off straightaway.

Willie was a hard-living Scot. Put a lager in his hand and anything could happen. But when you were going into battle there wasn't a better or braver man to have beside you.

We were in Kuwait and Pat Jennings was rooming with Willie. They were an unlikely couple to put together. Big Willie, as big Willie would, got hungry in the middle of the night. Most people at such an hour would turn over and go to sleep. Not Willie. He told Pat he was starving and was going off to find the kitchen. It was a new hotel and on the way back to the room with his tray of food, Willie fell down a ditch that had been freshly dug and nearly killed himself.

Willie would ruin five-a-side games. He was always fighting and arguing with Terry Neill. And they got on well! But Willie was a law unto himself. Don Howe, hard as he tried, could never make him out. Terry knew how to handle him. He could always get him in the right frame of mind to play – just as Don would start to despair.

We were doing pre-season in Heneff one year and John Crane, the club doctor, was conducting a fitness survey. It was an eight o'clock in the morning test. The doc would come to each room and have us stepping on and off a chair for 15 minutes to check our pulse rates before and after. He arrived at Willie's room and Willie refused, very colourfully, to let him in. Don was furious. But Willie was adamant. He was never at his best first thing in the morning.

Willie loved a battle – on or off the pitch. And he could look after himself. He looked after me too. He particularly enjoyed playing against Joe Jordan and Peter Withe . . . anyone who would give him a hard physical match. He didn't like players with good technique. His great strength was to stay in defensive positions and get everything away first time. He was particularly strong in the air. It allowed me the freedom to go forward.

I can truthfully say Willie never ever got me into trouble on or off the field. He spent four excellent years proving wrong a lot of people who doubted whether he had the ability to be

Back at Wembley. But we lost to West Ham. It wasn't a happy return.

an Arsenal player. In that respect, Willie would be the first to admit the debt he owed Don Howe.

Brian Clough signed Willie for Nottingham Forest and Don said, ''Cloughy won't know what has hit him. Willie will be his biggest test ever.'' I have a feeling another character, by the name of Stan Bowles, might just have surpassed Willie on that score. While he was at Arsenal, Willie was fined several times for disciplinary lapses. But everyone liked him.

Willie was no mug either. Linda, his wife, has a big equestrian centre, with 60 horses, just outside Nottingham. But Willie doesn't like horses and the last I heard he was running a hotel and bar up there. I am glad it appears to have gone well for him outside the game.

I played alongside Steve Walford for a while at Arsenal – though he was basically the deputy for both Willie and myself. Steve is a bit like Peter Simpson used to be. He has loads of ability, but he is easy going and not the best of competitors. I also got the feeling he was uncomfortable with big-club pressure.

Chris Whyte made his First Division debut alongside me against Manchester City in October 1981. We won 1-0 and there was a feeling he was in to stay. I had reservations. 'Huggy' was happy-go-lucky, always smiling. But he played his football the way he lived his life. He was always liable to make mistakes and it soon became clear he was not going to be the long-term answer to Willie Young's departure. 'Huggy' was a reasonable all-round player. But he lacked reliability. He stayed on the scene for two years and when I heard of him last season he was playing indoor soccer in America, before Ron Atkinson gave him another chance in League football at West Bromwich Albion.

Stewart Robson played alongside me at the back in that time too. Stewart did a good sound job. But he wasn't over-keen on playing there and central midfield was always going to be his best position. He only partnered me because we had nobody else.

In 1983–84, Colin Hill played alongside me. Again, it was a stop-gap job. Colin wasn't the answer. We were still looking for another Willie Young and it wasn't helping my game. As I say, central defenders go in pairs and I was finding it difficult getting used to the ways of a new partner every few games.

Terry Butcher was being linked with Arsenal in 1984, but nothing ever came of it. Finally, Tommy Caton joined us and for a time it looked good. Tommy wasn't the quickest. But we went well together. He was a good battler and very few strikers got the better of him in the air. Don was delighted with Tommy. When Viv Anderson arrived from Nottingham Forest in 1984 Arsenal's back four looked good. But suddenly, Tommy started to struggle. He used to worry about his lack of pace and I think it got him down. John Cartwright arrived as coach in 1985 and soon made it clear he didn't rate Tommy. He was left out of the side and never got back in. His game went backwards.

Tommy was a nice lad – but an awful worrier. You were always having to boost his confidence. He started to worry

The Greatest! Pele, with Brian Talbot and me at Highbury, where he was Arsenal's guest when we played Aston Villa.

about the crowd, claiming they didn't like him, and it all got on top of Tommy. It became essential for his peace of mind as well as his football that he moved on. Oxford bought Tommy, and it was a good move for him. Tommy was a real family man who liked his game of golf. Kenny Sansom was his best pal and it was a pity some of Kenny's immense self-confidence couldn't brush off on him.

Martin Keown played as my partner for the first time against Liverpool in December 1985 after Tommy was dropped. We won 2-0 and he looked the part. Martin had blistering pace but he was a lad who needed someone who wouldn't let him get too exposed. Concentration wasn't his strongest point. We stayed together for the rest of that season and I was sorry when he couldn't agree a new contract and left Arsenal for Aston Villa.

Keown came from Oxford and continued to live there when he got in the first team. He drove up and down every day. His first trip with Arsenal was when we went to play a midweek game in Trinidad. We left London on the Sunday and got there late in the evening. We were all tired but we were under orders to attend a big banquet arranged by the match sponsors. We sat down, had a meal, and waited for the speeches.

Some of the lads said to Martin, "It is the custom for the new player to respond at these dinners on behalf of the club." The head of the Trinidad Football Association spoke . . . then Martin got up and made a fantastic response. He had been set up but he had the last laugh.

Martin left for Villa after less than a season in Arsenal's first team and without George Graham ever seeing him play. But Martin was adamant that the money the club had offered him on a new contract just wasn't good enough.

Alf Fields, who used to help out with Arsenal's youth team, was insisting from the moment Tony Adams joined the club as a 16-year-old – at the time Chris Whyte was playing alongside me – that Tony would be my partner one day. I watch a lot of youth team matches and Tony at that time stood out. His enthusiasm for the game shone through. There was strength in his tackling, he was aggressive and he won everything in the air.

Even now, however, to be the complete central defender there are things I believe he needs to work on. His technique of passing the ball, for instance. He still tends to give it away. But that Tony has the potential to join the greats among England centre-halves is beyond argument. I have never seen a player have such an outstanding season after first coming into the side. I like to think, though, that coming into a back four that included Viv Anderson, Kenny Sansom and myself at that time would be a bit of a help to any youngster. I have since read an article quoting Luton manager Ray Harford in which he said a young player hoping to make his mark couldn't have been in a better, more organised back four.

But Tony is a confident lad. He wants to learn, he works at improving his game, and he has all the makings of someone who could go on to win a century of caps for his country.

One ranking list I can never see Tony reaching, however, is that of the country's ten best-dressed men. Before beating Liverpool in the Littlewoods Cup final in season 1986-87 we were invited into one of Bond Street's most exclusive shops and were told we could each pick any suit we wanted. 'Rodders' went for one that looked absolutely awful on him. He has got be the worst-dressed player in the club. Tony, I am afraid, is one of those people who will never look very tidy. It might help if he combed his hair now and again. He lives at home with his parents who are rightly very proud of him. He is the best partner I have ever had at the heart of Arsenal's defence and I hope we are going to be together for a long time to come.

It hasn't all been easy for Tony either. Just before George Graham arrived at Highbury, he suffered a hairline fracture of the shin-bone that put him out of football for six months.

At international level, I have partnered a number of outstanding central defenders. One of the unluckiest, because of recurring injuries, has been Kevin Moran. He is a Willie Young type of player . . . and more of a gentleman you couldn't wish to meet. Mick McCarthy I have always rated a good aggressive tackler who does particularly well against the Mick Harford type of centre-forward.

I have never actually played alongside Paul McGrath. When we have played together for the Republic he has always been in midfield. But he is a natural who obviously fits comfortably into most positions. Paul is strong as a bull, quick, and has excellent technique. It all comes almost too easy for him. Like Moran, he has been very unlucky with injuries. For a lad who has got a bit of a wild-man reputation off the pitch, he is the quietest fellow you could meet. He rarely makes a fuss, in fact he rarely talks, and is very easy to get on with.

If I have to name my partner of partners, it has to be Mark Lawrenson. He was the greatest . . . genuine world-class. Of course I am bound to be biased, but I happen to think that, for a while, Mark and I were the best international partnership around. I know that Ron Greenwood, when he was England manager, once said to me, "I wish the pair of you were playing for me . . . and you should be. You were both born in England." He said we would have been an automatic choice in his team.

It was a major disappointment to me that Eoin Hand broke the partnership up because he wanted to accommodate other players. Ironically, Mark's versatility didn't help. His ability to play equally well at right-back and in midfield made it easy for Eoin.

Mark was such a complete player. In the last couple of seasons, before injury brought such a tragic early end to a brilliant career, Mark rarely played at centre-back either for club or country. And I never ever heard him complain. In his view, the needs of the team came first. At Liverpool, it let in Gary Gillespie, and for the Republic the option of Mick McCarthy or Kevin Moran. I have to say I admired Mark tremendously. He always looked so comfortable on the ball. He had fantastic pace, was adequate in the air, was sharp and decisive with his tackling and had an enviable in-built confidence of his own ability.

Whenever we played Liverpool, I always made a point of having a drink with Mark after the game. I found him to be a really decent and honest person . . . someone who took pride in being a professional footballer. Someone who never abused the status it gave him.

The Achilles' tendon injury that finished Lawrenson was so sad. The last time he kicked a football in the First Division was against Arsenal at Anfield. Martin Hayes pushed a ball past Mark as if he wasn't there. Martin is quick, but that would never have happened in the old days. He signalled to the bench shortly afterwards that he wanted to come off . . . and never played again.

Three months later, Lawrenson announced his retirement and joined Oxford United as manager. As always, Mark and I had a drink after that last Anfield meeting. He said he wasn't right, and I knew he was struggling. His decision to quit was a loss to Liverpool, to Ireland and to football. The pity for me was that so much of his career was spent out of the position I always thought was his best – central defence. Even in that final game, he was at right-back.

Mark is relatively easy-going and I hope he develops the streak of toughness that is an essential ingredient for all

Togetherness, Arsenal's collection of Republic and Northern Ireland inter-nationals. From the front – Liam Brady, Pat Rice, John Devine, Sammy Nelson, Pat Jennings, Frank Stapleton and me.

managers. The best managers, after all, are not always the nicest people. When I look back I accept it was a pleasure and a privilege to have played alongside Mark for the Republic.

The nearest thing I have seen in English football to Franz Beckenbauer is Alan Hansen. His major strength is on the ball. His distribution is immaculate. I don't know of any defender in this country with the ability to start attacks from the back the way Hansen does. It helps, I suppose, being with Liverpool. Your best chance against him is in a one-to-one. But you don't often get that opportunity against Liverpool.

The best England centre-half of recent times has to be Terry Butcher. He is a big strong man who is a fearsome competitor. His very physical presence is intimidating. I felt very sorry for him at having to miss the European Championships. I know how he felt.

As for myself . . . I have always worn the number five shirt, while not being an out-and-out centre-half. Most of my years I have played as a second centre-half . . . complementing Willie Young, Tommy Caton, Mick McCarthy, Kevin Moran and now Tony Adams among others. They have been good years, years with plenty of variety, and I have no regrets.

CHAPTER TWENTY

Jack Charlton – The Truth

Jack Charlton hurt me more than any over-the-top tackle.

He accused me of not being interested in playing for my country. Nothing could be further from the truth. I have never felt so hurt or been insulted so deeply throughout my career.

I woke up one morning at the end of last season to headlines such as ''O'Leary is Finished Says Jack''. I couldn't believe it. I was shattered. For one thing, the timing could not have been worse. I had only just come out of hospital following an Achilles' tendon operation. But it went a lot deeper.

Over and over, I kept asking myself how could he say such a thing after my track record with the Republic of Ireland. I kept thinking of the international trips I had made with the Republic when others had made lame excuses and dropped out because they knew, as I did, that we were going away on little more than a glorified holiday.

I didn't know Jack Charlton before he became Ireland's manager. I knew only of his reputation . . . and that didn't exactly thrill me. He was, it seemed, pig-headed, stubborn and interested in no opinions other than his own. Players I knew who had worked with Charlton were hardly ecstatic about the way he wanted the game played. He didn't want defenders who thought about the game. He just wanted the ball played from back to front as quickly as possible.

The first time I met Charlton was after he had picked a squad to play Wales at Lansdowne Road. We all got together in Dublin on Monday 24 March 1986. It was a day I am unlikely to forget. One of the first things he said was, "All my life I have never regarded defenders as being able to play. You get the ball – and you get it away." This from a man who was a centre-half himself! I wasn't his sort of player – that was obvious.

I would like to think there are enough people in the game who would support my own belief that I am not a defender who just boots the ball away. I am not a tough-guy centre-half and certainly not one in the Jack Charlton kick-it-anywhere school. I hope not, anyway.

I played in that first match of the Charlton régime, against Wales. The instructions were for the defenders not to pass across the back, to forget about playing ten-yard balls . . . and to get it forward into the last third of the field as quickly as possible. We lost 1-0. I was partially to blame for the goal, but I thought I played well. I was the defender on the near post when a corner was flicked on for Ian Rush to score at the far post. I was a bit annoyed with myself. Charlton said to me later, "I thought you should have done better with that near post ball." It was fair comment. He was right. I knew that.

He had me wondering about him on the Monday we met up before the Wales game. We went in for lunch and he came and sat next to me. He talked generally about taking the Irish job and that he wasn't getting much for doing it. He then said he had seen Arsenal play at Newcastle. He remarked of Kenny Sansom, "Your left-back . . . He passes it here, he passes it there . . . Does Don Howe not say anything to him?" He was talking about the best left-back in England – a player with 60 caps at that time.

It was prior to that Wales game, when Jack Charlton was outlining the way that he saw things, that he observed, "Even if you are struggling with injury, I expect you to get over here and report for international duty." Immediately, I thought there is no way Arsenal will ever allow an unfit player to go off to an international. I also found it an interesting observation from one of Don Revie's former Leeds United players.

Ireland's next game under Charlton was against Uruguay. I was named in the squad. But three weeks before the game, I pulled a hamstring. It happened in the last minute of a match with Watford . . . on the Monday following the Irish defeat against Wales. John Crane, Arsenal's doctor, said it was a fatigue injury – the sort you get at the end of a long, hard season – and it would take a few weeks to clear up.

A week before the Uruguay international, Steve Burtenshaw, who was now Arsenal's acting manager following the shock departure of Don Howe, said he didn't think I would be right for the international. In fact, I didn't play for Arsenal again until 26 April against West Bromwich – three days after the Uruguay match. I was out for a month.

On 16 April, Arsenal had played Sheffield Wednesday at Hillsborough. I wasn't fit to play, but I travelled with the team specifically in the hope of seeing Jack Charlton. I

Trophy time again. Collecting a statuette after winning my 25th Republic of Ireland cap, against Holland in Dublin.

thought he might be at the game and I would be able to explain the hamstring was 99 per cent certain to keep me out against Uruguay. He wasn't there.

Afterwards, Steve Burtenshaw, knowing I was concerned, said he would get in touch with Mr Charlton. He tried to telephone him, but told me later he just could not track Jack down. He added I shouldn't worry. He had contacted the Football Association of Ireland and left a message to say he couldn't get in touch with Jack Charlton but David O'Leary was injured and unable to make the squad.

The Republic played Uruguay and a few days later I was at a function to raise money to build a hostel for down-and-outs. I met Gerry Ryan, the former Brighton star. He had just come back from Ireland and he told me, "They are not too pleased with you over there. They were waiting for you to turn up." As I was driving home that night it occurred to me they might not have got the message I was being withdrawn because of injury. I started to think about Jack Charlton's remark at that first meeting . . . about getting over even if you were struggling with injury.

I went in to see Steve Burtenshaw the following morning and said, "I don't think they got the message."

He replied, "Don't be silly. Of course they did."

I retorted, "We'll see when the next squad comes out."

Steve looked at me and said, "You're being stupid. They are not going to leave you out. They know what has happened."

The next scheduled international was a tournament in Iceland at the end of May. I played against Oxford United on 5 May, our last League game, knowing I had to keep in training after that because of the Iceland trip. At the same time I repeated to Steve, "I don't think Jack Charlton is going to pick me."

A few days later I came back from a training run one morning and Joy, my wife, said, "The phone hasn't stopped ringing. The calls are all saying you have been dropped by the Republic for the first time ever." Joy then made the point, "We could have been away on holiday. Perhaps we can plan a family break now."

I didn't hear from Jack Charlton and I am not suggesting for one moment that it was part of his job to give me an explanation of why I had been left out. But I was still very disappointed as I went ahead and arranged to go away with the family.

I spoke to Liam Brady on the phone in Italy to ask whether he would be able to play in my testimonial. Typically, he said he would do his best to make it. We chatted briefly, and I said, "Good luck for the Iceland trip."

Liam said he was sorry I wasn't in the squad and asked whether Jack Charlton had contacted me with any explanation. When I told him 'No', Liam joked, "It's probably because you pass the ball."

I was out with my two children, John and Ciara on the day Liverpool beat Everton in the 1986 FA Cup final. We got home and Joy said, "Jack Charlton has been on the phone. He will ring you later."

He telephoned again on the following Monday morning. There were no preliminaries. He said, "David, a few players have pulled out." I thought to myself . . . that's an understatement. He went on, "Could you be at Heathrow Airport to join up with the squad for Iceland?"

I thought there and then to ask why I had been left out in the first place. Deep down I was furious. I knew he was using me. He was calling because other players had let him down with so-called injuries . . . injuries that wouldn't have borne too close examination. I felt very hurt by the way he had gone about things. I hadn't heard a word about why I had been dropped. Now, suddenly, he needed me. I wasn't going to be his lackey! So I told him the truth. I pointed out I had made arrangements to go away. I said I had done nothing about a family holiday until the squad was announced. When I wasn't in, I planned my summer.

He said, "That means you won't be at the airport?"

I replied, "That's right."

The phone went dead. It was the last time we spoke.

Maurice Setters is the man Jack Charlton made his assistant after settling into the Republic job. I have never met Setters.

At least, I don't think I have. Certainly, he doesn't appear to know who I am.

Setters has been to a lot of Arsenal games, and to my knowledge has been in our dressing-room a couple of times – once at Doncaster and once at Sheffield Wednesday. Each time it was to see Niall Quinn. I am assuming it was to see Niall. On both occasions it was Niall he spoke to. Me? I was ignored completely. It saddened me. After all, this was the fellow who was reporting back to the manager. It became clear, as the European Championship qualifiers reached their climax and the finals drew near, that it would take the mass withdrawal of every Irish defender before I figured in their plans.

I had played 40 times for my country. Charlton and Setters had been involved with the Republic for two minutes. What did they know about what playing for Ireland meant to me?

The season moved on and Arsenal played Tottenham in a televised Sunday match at Highbury. We beat our biggest rivals 2-1, with Perry Groves getting the winner. I was struggling with my Achilles' tendon injury by then and didn't play. I walked into the marble halls before the game and spotted Ted Buxton, who is Tottenham's chief scout. I have known Ted for years. I went over to talk to him. Who was standing with Ted? Maurice Setters. As I drew near, Setters turned his back on me and started to talk to someone else. I stood chatting with Ted for about five minutes. In that time, Setters didn't turn round once. Am I being over-sensitive? I don't think so. Frankly I found the scene embarrassing. Confusing, too.

A couple of weeks earlier, George Graham came back from watching Sheffield Wednesday play Everton. He had seen Setters there, who had said to him: "Tell David O'Leary that the story in the Irish papers about me blanking him in the Arsenal dressing-room is untrue. It wasn't deliberate. I didn't snub him." Nothing, now, however, was going to convince me otherwise after what had just happened. I have since been told that the real reason Maurice doesn't talk to me is that he says he doesn't know me. It just gets odder and odder.

North and South get together. Arsenal's Northern Ireland star Pat Rice and me at Highbury.

Jack Charlton might not have included me in his European Championship plans, but at least he was aware of my existence. When we played at Newcastle, half the team were waiting outside afterwards for the coach to pull up. They were building a new stand last season and it was difficult to know where to go after coming out of the dressing-room. I came out later, the coach was there, and I got straight on. David Rocastle said to me, "Jack Charlton was asking after you."

I responded, "What do you mean?"

David said, "Well, he went up to John Lukic and said, 'Hullo David. Good result.'"

John, I was told later, turned round and said "It's not Dave." Jack, I believe, acknowledged his mistake and said, "Give Dave my regards."

I repeat that not one word passed between Charlton and myself between the time he put the phone down on me and Ireland going off to play in the European Championship finals. I went into hospital for my Achilles' operation, and if there was any message from Jack it didn't reach me. The only word I have had from the Republic's manager has reached me through Arsenal's assistant manager, Theo Foley, who told me that Charlton had said to him he didn't rate me as a player.

I find myself returning to Jack Charlton's accusation that I am not interested in my country. I can only stress that in the decade-and-a-half I have spent at the top it is the most hurtful and inaccurate comment ever aimed at me. My mum and dad telephoned from Dublin the day after reading his comments. They were bitterly upset. Every time I was picked for my country, they were so proud. They never tired of telling me how good they felt when I put on the green jersey of Ireland and they stood at Lansdowne Road as the National Anthem was played. I want people to understand why I felt so bitter towards Charlton.

When the England season finishes, I have a holiday and spend my summers in Ireland. I would like to think that finding an Irishman who reckons I don't love my country is on a par with finding a pub in the Republic that doesn't sell Guinness.

I admired and respected what Jack achieved as an England player. There can be no greater honour in the game than winning the World Cup. I know I would not dare suggest that he was not interested in playing for his country. But I must now judge him on the way he treated me.

Loyalty? Ask successive Arsenal managers. I have been at Highbury 15 years – and never once asked for a transfer. No Republic manager prior to Jack Charlton ever remotely criticised my attitude.

In the eyes of so many people, Charlton came home from West Germany in June 1988 as a winner. I happen to think the game of football was the loser. If humping the ball forward from the back and playing the Charlton way is what it's all about, then the majority of the world's most admired footballers will soon be redundant. Once you throw skill out of the window, soccer becomes a second-class sport.

I watched every match of the European Championship on television, and the Republic of Ireland had no bigger fan than me. I cheered myself hoarse when we beat England. I was delighted with the draw against Russia . . . and devastated by the defeat against Holland. I badly wanted to be there . . . but an operation at the worst possible time and a manager who probably didn't see me as fitting into his plans anyway, dictated otherwise. The warm feeling I felt for my country last summer did not extend to Jack Charlton.

Looking back, do I regret not cancelling my holiday that fateful day and going with Ireland to Iceland? The answer is a definite, unqualified 'No'. I would do the same all over again. I know I wasn't in the wrong. What Jack Charlton thinks is up to him.

The manager will always win. I was always going to be the loser. I knew that from the moment Jack Charlton put the phone down on me. I know this will not help my chances of being selected for the World Cup qualifiers. But the time has come to state my case. In the past two years I have been offered a lot of money to tell my side of the story. I always refused. Am I a troublemaker? I would like to think the facts suggest otherwise. I have never been fined by my club and I have never before fallen out with a manager.

What I have said is the truth of an unhappy situation as I saw it. I am glad I have got it off my chest.

CHAPTER TWENTY-ONE

A Player's View

Referees, fans, television, the Press . . . all are an essential part
of the great game. I have never been anti-Press, appreciate the
excitement television generates and accept that referees have
the least enviable job in soccer. They can never win.

Thinking about it, I do not know of one ex-professional
who has turned seriously to refereeing once his playing days
were over. I cannot even recall any ex-pro giving the idea
serious consideration. That is a great pity. In industry after
all, the foreman always comes off the shop floor. There is no
better way of understanding the job the men are doing.

There is a feeling among older players that present refereeing standards are not what they used to be. But then, I
suppose, the senior pros ten and 20 years ago were saying the
same thing. For all that, I feel there isn't the strength in depth
of outstanding refs that there used to be. These days, you see
the same faces at all the top games. I also know that if I look
at the programme and see Keith Hackett or George Courtney
is 'doing' our game, I am happy. They are referees for whom
I have the highest regard. They are what I call players' refs.
You can speak to them knowing that as long as you are not
being silly or abusive you will be treated in a civilised manner.

Neither is pompous. Both are down to earth. Players can relate to them . . . knowing they will let you know soon enough when you have gone outside the rules.

It is when you go to Anfield and Old Trafford that you need a referee in the Keith Hackett, George Courtney mould. The really good referees will not be influenced by either the imposing stadium or the partisanship of the crowd.

I remember Alex Ferguson remarking that, when you go to Anfield, you need a miracle. Up to a point, I can understand what he means. It is not Liverpool's fault that they have got fanatical fans and a team that drives forward all the time. For a young referee that can be an intimidating combination.

At Anfield, you can be down near the corner flag and the ball goes out of play. It is a goal kick. But 20,000 fans massed on the Kop roar, "Corner". The referee is 20 yards away and the linesman has not had a clear view. What would you do? It can be the same thing with penalties. Is it really coincidence that Liverpool get so many at Anfield? I wouldn't mind – but Liverpool are so good anyway.

Players often say that when you are sitting in the dug-out, the hot-dog man will walk past and be cheering and shouting for Liverpool louder than any fan on the Kop. He has also been known to look down at where we are sitting and say, "You've no chance today."

Getting even a point at Anfield is reason to celebrate all the way back to London. Not that Old Trafford is much easier for the away side . . . or the referee.

Generally, over the years, I have had a good relationship with referees. I understand they cannot please everyone and have always tried to bite my tongue when I have felt they were wrong. At least referees in this country are totally honest. When they give what I think might be an incorrect decision, it is a genuine mistake.

But one referee I could never get on with was Roger Kirkpatrick, from Leicester. I found him a world away from people like Hackett, Courtney and Lester Shapter. He was unbelievably arrogant. I once tried politely to make a point to him in a First Division game. He looked at me and said, "You talk . . . you walk." I was disgusted.

Down the years it has been suggested that referees would be better if, like players, they did the job full-time. I cannot see why. What bothers me is that there appears to be a widening gulf between referees and players. It has become them and us. I would like to see them have more contact with their local clubs, train there, have discussion groups, try to develop a better understanding. Surely the Professional Footballers' Association and the League Referees' Association could be doing more in this respect. It hasn't helped, either, the way the pace of the game has stepped up a gear in recent years. It means referees need to be fitter than they ever have in the past.

I do firmly believe, however, that referees – and linesmen – are underpaid. They can win you a Cup, cost you a League. Their responsibility is enormous. One decision can make or break your season. Even though more money wouldn't mean better referees, they ought to be more amply rewarded.

Chris Waddle and I battle it out in the first leg of the Littlewoods Cup semi-final. Spurs won this one but we got to Wembley.

But above all there has to be a better understanding. More liaison, not less, between referees and players can surely only help us understand each other's problems better. I accept that if you swear directly at a referee you cannot complain at being booked or even sent off. But at the moment we are not allowed to question a referee's decision. It is regarded as dissent and I am not sure that is right.

Difficult as it is to win at Old Trafford, I have to say I love playing there. Next, of course, to Highbury, I think it is my favourite ground. The stadium is in a class of its own. For a feeling of tradition and something special I would have to say it matches Anfield and Highbury. When I was a youngster, having just come into the game, I don't think any stadium gave me a bigger thrill when I stepped out to play than Old Trafford. It has the aura of a world-famous club. The pitch, the stands, the executive suites, the facilities for players after a game. All are top-class. Even the away dressing-room, which didn't used to be the best, is excellent now.

There are other clubs and grounds that have always impressed me. Everton, particularly in the 1986–87 season, come into that category. Everton are one of those clubs whose players don't give out tickets to the opposing team's guests for the players' lounge after the game. For that reason, they can't expect tickets in return when they come to Highbury. It works both ways. Last season, when we played there in the semi-final of the Littlewoods Cup, that situation presented me with a bit of a problem. My dad had come over from Dublin and I got changed as quickly as possible after the match to find him. One of the Everton stewards came in just as I was leaving the dressing-room to say my dad had been taken to one of the executive suites and was being looked after. I was very grateful.

A lot of the fans think that Arsenal and Tottenham players wouldn't be seen dead in each other's company. Nothing could be further from the truth. We all get along very well . . . other than on match days! Glenn Hoddle, when he was at Tottenham, and Graham Rix, while he was at Arsenal, were, for instance, particularly close friends.

Tottenham has always struck me as being a very well run club. Certainly, there is always a terrific atmosphere at White Hart Lane when it is derby day against Arsenal. I want to see them doing well. Nothing in the First Division beats the rivalry between Liverpool and Everton fans. But in the fan 'war' game, Arsenal and Tottenham are not far behind. I don't mind it if Spurs are FA Cup finalists . . . as long as it is Arsenal who walk off Wembley with the Cup. I am delighted for Spurs to finish First Division runners-up . . . as long as we are champions.

As a club, they are definitely near the top in the hospitality league. Arsenal players, when they go to watch a game at White Hart Lane, are always well looked after. You get car park space, a good seat and an invitation to come in and have a drink after the match. When we beat Spurs in the Littlewoods Cup semi-final at White Hart Lane, Irving Scholar, the Tottenham chairman, sent a crate of champagne into our dressing-room. I thought that was a touch of class.

I always enjoy going up to Tyneside to play Newcastle. The crowd there are fantastic. It can be wet, it can be windy, it can be bitterly cold. The fans might have no cover over them, and their team can be struggling. But the fervour of the supporters is something else. No side could ask for a better, more loyal support. And they know the game. One of the things I have never been able to understand is why some top players are reluctant to go to Newcastle or, when they do, appear reluctant to stay.

The Dell is a ground I definitely don't like. I have nothing against the club or their fans. But the stadium is so tight. It is a bits-and-pieces ground, with the crowd right on top of you. It is hard to raise your game. Derby County is similar to Southampton. Cramped, and with a poor playing surface. But the crowd atmosphere is great. It remains, however, one of those places where you go and are glad to get away from as quickly as possible. The same, I am afraid, applies to Watford.

Across the border in Scotland, Rangers and Celtic, for support, tradition and stadiums dripping with atmosphere, can give most English clubs a start and still beat them. Ibrox, certainly, is special – with its cantilever stands, banks of seats and facilities to match anything in Europe. It is not a hospitable place to many players, but it still has a certain, magical splendour.

Back in England, Queen's Park Rangers has once again become a ground pleasant to visit. It has always been a neat, spotlessly clean stadium. I am delighted they have pulled up that dreadful artificial pitch. I am just sorry Luton have not followed them. Why Rangers were ever allowed to lay it in the first place has to be something of a mystery. It set an unfortunate trend. And I cannot agree it is in the name of progress. Football should be played on grass. There is no substitute.

The World Cup, the European Championship, the European club competitions. They are all played on grass. Rightly so. I am very much against artificial surfaces. I do not know a player who isn't. The clubs who have them tell you they bring in extra revenue. They argue, too, that you can play on plastic come rain, snow or frost. But it is how you can play that is surely important. I believe games on artificial pitches are themselves artificial. The bounce of the ball is a joke. You fall on plastic and you are cut to pieces. You go for a sliding tackle and you are left with bad and painful burns. Goalkeepers have to pad up as if they are going out to play American football. I have come away from Queen's Park Rangers and Luton in the past and been stiff as a board the following day. When we played at both grounds, their physiotherapist would come in before the game with a special cream to administer to the burns we were certain to get. If Luton were to follow Rangers and go back to natural grass, I am sure players throughout the country would be delighted.

After the tragedy of the Heysel Stadium disaster, it was right that English clubs should be banned from Europe. It was the only way to show the hooligan minority who fester our game that their disgraceful behaviour was making them outcasts.

I accept that what happened at the European Championships was not the best advert for the English fan. But I am among those who believe we have paid the price. A tremendous effort has been made by clubs to curb the mindless louts who use football as a way to exploit violence. The heavy policing of football grounds is now something that will never go away. Unfortunately, Colin Moynihan has been just one in a lengthening line of sports ministers who jumped on the bandwagon . . . eager to denounce violence, but without much idea of how to stop it. I feel he watches his football from the House of Commons.

Television, radio and Press coverage often doesn't help either. I am not suggesting crowd trouble should be swept under the carpet. But it should not be exploited either.

Generally, television's coverage of games is very good, though I find there is an increasing tendency among certain commentators to impose their views rather than report what they see. There are times when they try to be too technical. They will go into detail about a particular tactic when I would question whether they really understand it.

A lot of people, and that includes some players, knock the *Saint and Greavesie* show on ITV. I have done a couple of coaching sessions in Ireland with Jimmy Greaves. Not only is he great with kids, but he has also got good and sensible views on the game. Anyway, when I was a kid, he was one of my idols!

I have always had a reasonable relationship with the Press. If I can help, I will. If I am asked a genuine question, I always try to give a genuine answer, Reporters know that frivolous gossip is not my game . . . neither is knocking other players. Like most players I trust some reporters more than I do others. But then trust and distrust applies to all walks of life.

That relations between football and the Press could be better doesn't get an argument from me. There is mistrust on both sides. Yet I have to say I see a disturbing trend in the popular Press. It was highlighted at the height of Chelsea's troubles last season. The papers gave me the impression they were going out looking for former players who would attack the club that once gave them a good living. I know that reporters have to work to tight deadlines. But it still annoys

me, as it does most players, to see myself quoted in a newspaper when I have not even spoken to the journalist whose
name appears on the article. I wouldn't mind if I was told that
what I had said was being passed on.

On weekdays, we always have the *Daily Mail* delivered at
home. On Sundays, it is the *Mail on Sunday* and the *News of
the World*. Usually, I will go into the newsagent and buy *The
Observer*. Certain sportswriters, I particularly enjoy. Hugh
McIlvanney, Ian Wooldridge and Patrick Collins come into
that category. There is little doubt in my mind, though, that
even if they don't have the paper at home, most footballers
see the *Sun* at some stage during the day. While their football
coverage can border on the sensational, it is the paper where
you will often find the big stories.

Going back to what happened at Chelsea in the 1987–88
season, it saddens me when players go out of the game then
for money allow articles to be written in their name attacking
clubs and players in situations where they cannot possibly
have the full facts. It is depressing to see ex-players having to
earn money that way.

Like a lot of my fellow professionals I receive regular
invitations to sit on sports panels. When I can oblige, I do.
The questions reflect the interest the countless genuine fans
take in all aspects of our national game. I am often asked
whether we should have a super league. In fact, the Football
League have made a commendable effort to reduce the size
of the First Division. I happen to think they could go still
further. It is my personal opinion that the ideal First Division
would be made up of no more than 18 clubs. I think we ask
too much of our top professional players. How are we ever
going to match the technique we admire so much in other
countries when our managers and coaches have so little time
in the week to work with players on their skills?

My own club Arsenal was involved in talks during the
summer that appear to suggest that the eventual formation of
a super league is not far away. It has got to come. We already
have a situation where it is difficult each season to look past
five or six clubs to find the eventual League champions. Based

on crowd-pulling power, tradition and past achievements this would be my 18-club super division if I wake up one day to find myself football's dictator: Arsenal, Aston Villa, Chelsea, Derby County, Everton, Liverpool, Leeds United, Manchester United, Manchester City, Newcastle United, Nottingham Forest, Sheffield Wednesday, Sunderland, West Ham, Tottenham, QPR, Southampton and Luton. I make that 18-strong nomination with apologies to my many mates at clubs such as Coventry, Charlton and Wolves.

Another question that gets a regular airing is what rule I would most like to see changed. Frankly, I find the present offside law as frustrating as losing a derby game against Tottenham. So many matches are spoilt by disputes over whether or not a player was offside when he scored a crucial goal. Was he, for instance, interfering with play? I think it infuriates both fans and players. And it is getting harder and harder for linesmen.

All the good sides, Liverpool, Everton and Arsenal, use the offside law to our advantage. You can't blame us. But it

Lining up for the 1977-78 season.

means the game is played in fits and starts. What I would like to see is no offside up to the penalty box. Extend the 18-yard line right across the pitch. It would open up the game, allow players to express themselves. Skill would flourish. As it is, you push up, keep everything compact and tight . . . and find you are playing in one-third of the field. So many of the debates you see on television following a big match concern a disputed offside.

Very recently, I was asked to name my all-time team of Arsenal greats . . . the best I have played with in my 15 memorable years with the club. That particular questioner named David O'Leary. I am sure it was to save me from embarrassment. With apologies to many fine players who deserve to be there, this was my answer:

PAT JENNINGS – The greatest goalkeeper of my era, Better, I believe, than Peter Shilton. He was a natural. He had great presence, always stayed cool. Defenders took it for granted that he would be there when needed.

VIV ANDERSON – He just gets the nod over Pat Rice . . . mainly because of his willingness to get forward and score important goals. He was one of the worst trainers I have ever known – but also among the fittest of men on a match day. He couldn't run during the week but didn't know how to stop on a Saturday.

DAVID O'LEARY – I leave others to judge. Anyway who picked this team?

TONY ADAMS – A lad with an outstanding attitude. He is full of confidence. He always wants to win the ball and is very good in the air. The ideal defensive partner. But Willie Young and Peter Simpson come into the frame.

KENNY SANSOM – A great player for Arsenal and a great player for England. But he only just edges out Bob McNab. While he is on the small side, Kenny has great spring in his jump. He is also very composed on the ball and a first-class defender. Amazingly, Kenny doesn't tackle. He doesn't need to. He reads it so well he gets to the ball first. Kenny jokes, "You get hurt if you tackle."

GEORGE ARMSTRONG – His heart was bigger than him.

But what a player. He was a footballing workaholic and one of the best team players I have ever known. In a couple of years time my vote could go to David Rocastle. Like George, he is very brave. He has the additional advantage of being blessed with the John Barnes type of natural ability.

ALAN BALL – The best one-touch player I have ever seen. He was the tops as a give-it-and-go-man. Also very bubbly. Got others around him to play. Alan Hudson wasn't that far behind. I often felt he would have been a better player in Italy or Spain.

LIAM BRADY – The ace playmaker . . . truly world-class. His right leg was for standing on, but his left is like a magic wand. It is an exciting sight when he goes at people with that deceptive turn of pace.

CHARLIE GEORGE – I would have him playing off my front two. He had two great feet and was always liable to score spectacular goals. Perhaps with a better attitude and if he had been less prone to injury, Charlie would have been one of the game's all-time greats.

FRANK STAPLETON – Just gets in ahead of John Radford, who was a terrific leader of the line with a good touch for a big man. But Frank was that fraction better at all the things Raddy excelled at. He was also totally unselfish.

ALAN SUNDERLAND – He was the perfect partner for Frank. He had a wonderful touch on the ball, was brave, and I always felt he was at his best if a defender kicked him early on. I was a fan of Malcolm Macdonald, because he was such a marvellous marksman. But on the basis of my belief that the best strikers hunt in pairs, I narrowly go for Sunderland.

If you were me, wouldn't you want to be part of a team like that!

CHAPTER TWENTY-TWO

The Future

So what of the future? What will I do when the decision is made – either by me or someone else – to bring an end to my days as a player?

My present contract finishes on 2 May 1991, my 33rd birthday. I would like, as I have already said, to play on for a further two years at the top with Arsenal. But that will be up to the club as much as it will be me. I understand and accept that.

My feeling right now is that I would like to stay in the game when I finally finish as a player. Many I know say that. Not that many get the chance. If an opportunity came my way I would want the right people with me. When you start out on the managerial road I believe it is essential to have by your side an older more experienced man who knows the problems and the pitfalls . . someone you can turn to, lean on and learn from.

Mark Lawrenson, a good friend from our times together in the Republic of Ireland side, got his chance at Oxford after injury had wrecked one of the game's most illustrious careers. They were facing relegation and needing a miracle which they didn't get to stay up. It was a tough beginning.

Home sweet home. Joy, our children Cara and John, and the family dog Kelly.

Mark went in there on his own – not able to take anyone from Liverpool, where he spent his best years as a player. He couldn't ask someone like Roy Evans or Bob Paisley to go with him. They were not going to leave Anfield. That is where Kenny Dalglish was lucky when he became player-manager. He inherited the best backroom team in football. The structure was already there. But then how many Liverpools are there? There isn't another club in the country – except possibly West Ham – who can boast of the same sort of continuity. They are like a well-maintained, custom-built car. Everything runs smoothly. Now and again they change the driver – but he is always a man who has served his apprenticeship at the Anfield factory for fine football.

Would I fancy being a player-manager one day? I might. But I have been told, and I have seen, just how tough the dual role can be. Johnny Giles, when he was player-manager of West Bromwich Albion, told me at the time that he didn't realise how hard it would be. You have to maintain your fitness, but when you get to the age of around 35 you need your rest too. A player-manager, however, doesn't just play and conduct the training sessions. You also have to go looking for players and assess other teams. I feel it is asking too much. It is strenuous enough being a player – never mind a manager. Combining the two strikes me as a near impossibility. And the lower down the scale you go, the harder it is going to be. These days, more than ever, clubs are looking to economise. They cannot afford a big staff.

John Hollins is a good friend of mine. When we were together at Arsenal, I always saw him as a future manager. He had a neat appearance – and that always impresses directors – he spoke well about the game, he had the right attitude and was never in any sort of trouble. He was, I suppose, the perfect professional . . . well-liked and with just the right image.

But did I think he would be a success as a manager? I had my doubts. He didn't impress me that much with his tactical knowledge and I felt he often was not positive enough. When John became manager of Chelsea, I thought that came through in his team selections. He seemed to chop and change a lot, without ever getting a settled side.

I believe that, when it comes to team building, you have to start at the back. As obvious as that might seem, there are some managers who see it differently. If you don't get a decent system for your back four, you are going to struggle. That, to me, always appeared to be Chelsea's problem. Yet I know John worked 16 and 17 hours a day to get it right. I also know the job changed him . . . got on top of him. From being someone who was always chirpy and happy-go-lucky he became withdrawn and you could see the strain had got to him. I found that sad. At Arsenal, there was no bigger enthusiast than John. He loved the game and he was always helping people. Yet when he was at Chelsea, Linda, his wife, used to say to me, "Never be a manager, Dave. Only if it is the last job on earth."

Many of the managers I have met say the same thing. But it must be some sort of drug. Whenever a job is advertised, you usually get 200 people chasing it – most of them friends of the poor guy who has just got the sack.

I look back on Don Howe's days at Arsenal. The golden days were those when he was coach. On that side of the job he is in the front rank of the best of the best. I can't help feeling, though, that he needs a Bertie Mee, a Bobby Gould or a Terry Neill – when those two were functioning as a terrific team – taking the strain of the paperwork, the Press calls, the contract discussions and the office routine. As a manager at Arsenal and West Bromwich before that, Don wasn't a success. But as a coach . . . different class.

To be fair, Don has mellowed. He seems to have a more open mind now. It makes him easier to talk to, easier to get on with. It could be what was missing before. Certainly, I would love to see him succeed as a manager. Whether he would fancy the challenge again after his heart operation in the summer is something else.

Don, at one stage last season, was being touted to follow John Hollins at Chelsea. I was glad that Bobby Campbell got his chance. When I first knew him, he was first-team coach at Arsenal. It was a pleasure then to work for him. I know there were those who didn't get on with Bobby, but I had no complaints. He was first-class at building up young players, giving them confidence, making them feel good. And isn't that an important part of coaching and man management?

If the chance ever comes to be a manager, one of the things I would do before even considering acceptance, would be to ask for a rundown on all the players' contracts. If there are dodgy characters I would want to know the length of their contracts. I would want them out at the first opportunity. I would not want to inherit players with two and three years to go who were going to cause me problems. That would be two or three years of aggro. Players like that can poison the atmosphere in a club, make it impossible to build up team spirit.

And, of course, I would want my own right-hand man – someone who would be happy to pass on his experience and knowledge to a young upstart. Unfortunately, it is not a perfect world. If it were, I would invite the backroom staff that Kenny Dalglish inherited to join me.

All of the managers I have played for at Arsenal have had their own particular strengths. Bertie Mee was the master organiser. He was the overlord of everything when he managed Arsenal. That was scouting, coaching, player recruitment – the lot. He was in complete command, supervising every facet of the day-to-day running of the club. A young manager would find it hard not to be successful if he had Bertie by his side. I always thought it was a master stroke by Graham Taylor to take him to Watford.

Terry Neill's big strength was Don Howe, and that is no exaggeration. His other strength was that he knew his own weaknesses and limitations. He appointed a coach and allowed him to express himself totally on the training field. That was brave as well as sensible.

I learned something else from Terry – if rather indirectly. I learned that nothing infuriates players more than a waffler. If you need to tell a player something . . . tell it to him straight. Don't go all round the houses. If it is about a contract, if it is to tell him he had a rubbish match, or you have to drop him – be straight. Players won't respect you otherwise.

One of the things I liked about Don Howe was his honesty. In my own dealings with him, I always thought that what he said was what he felt and what was best for me. Don used to hammer home to us, "This game isn't only about the money you can get out of it. It is about ambition too . . . ambition to win medals." He was right. But one of the things I didn't like when I first knew him was that I believed Don could be a bit of a training-ground bully. Perhaps, though, there is something to be said for that too.

With George Graham, one of his great strengths is that he has never forgotten he was a player himself. Some managers do. A problem will arise, and the boss sorts it out rationally. He will make his point, and that will be it. He will not harp on it the next day. I like that. Mind you, I think he could be ruthless if the occasion demanded it. Experience, however, has taught me that to be a successful manager, a touch of ruthlessness is necessary.

Those at the top now know there are young men who have just switched to the managerial side who will very soon be ready and able to take their jobs from them. Gerry Francis, the former England captain, is one up-and-coming manager who has impressed me as someone to watch for in the future. He speaks well about the game, seems to know what he wants and has a system that is positive. I liked the way he went about things last summer. Many of us in the game knew he had received offers from other, bigger clubs. Not only did he decide to continue his education with Bristol Rovers, where he did a fine job in the 1987–88 season with no money to spend on players, but he refused to name the clubs who had come in for him. That showed both consideration and character.

A future manager of England when Bobby Robson decides to call it a day? I have a sneaking regard for Graham Taylor in that direction . . . even though there are times when I think he shows a certain arrogance that does not endear you to the man.

One other young manager has impressed me – Steve

Perryman at Brentford. I had a high regard for him as a player who thought very deeply about the game at Tottenham and I feel he is serving his managerial apprenticeship quietly and without fuss at Griffin Park.

I know this. If I ever do make it to be a manager, I would like the sort of chairman I have played for at Arsenal. I would know that if I failed it would be my own fault. I wouldn't be able to blame an interfering chairman.

Also, if it didn't work out for me as a manager, I think I can say I wouldn't be on the dole. Anything I have earned from football, I have tried to look after. Perhaps I have been lucky as well as careful. I had the good fortune to meet Michael Kennedy and Tony Beatty early on in my career. Michael is a solicitor and Tony an accountant. I play my football and they look after what it earns me. They are friends. They have never taken even one per cent out of what I get. I was in Arsenal's first team at 17 and I have known them both almost since then. One of the first things they advised me against was flashy cars. They said bricks and mortar go up in value . . . cars go down.

On their advice, I bought my first house when I was 18. I have tried to buy a better one every few years since then. From the age of 18, too, I have invested in a pension fund . . . fully aware that the big earning days won't last for ever.

I cannot see myself running a corner shop or working in a garage. That is not in any way meant to degrade or detract from friends I have who do just that. But it isn't me. I have seen so many people come out of the game with nothing. I am determined to try to make sure that it doesn't happen to me.

Certainly, I couldn't have a better friend or adviser than Michael Kennedy. I have been very lucky. The day I met him was one of the most important in my life.

It hits home when I hear and read of great former players such as John Charles, Stan Bowles, Tony Currie and Peter Osgood having a hard time of it. I know of one former international star who regularly calls on the PFA to help him pay his gas and electricity bills.

I think the PFA do a great job . . . particularly in making

sure professional footballers know what they face when their careers end. They advise you on pension schemes and run many different courses – even including learning to be a pilot – while paying three-quarters of the cost. And all this for £20 a year. Tell me any other union that looks after its members so well.

Without meaning to be harsh, I feel any top player who finishes up broke has only himself to blame. Too many players get mixed up with the hangers on who are an unfortunate part of top-class football and pay for it later on. These people are nothing other than leeches who want to know a player when he is famous then discard him once his career goes into decline. Perhaps I have been lucky with those who have been close to me. Certainly, I have had my share of sharpies putting up schemes they guarantee will make me a fortune overnight. I have never got involved.

I have never had an agent either. I once got wined and dined by the Mark McCormack organisation. The courtship went on for six months. It started when Liam Brady and I were invited to meet them at their offices in London. They told us they were moving into soccer and asked if we would be interested in joining them. They said they wanted a string of a dozen top English, Scottish, Irish and Welsh players across the country. I have to say I was impressed. I would have happily joined their organisation, but I don't think they could come to terms with football being run on very different lines from golf, tennis and motor racing. In those sports, there is vast money to be earned from individual sponsorships and the touting, particularly in front of the television cameras, of company logos. They didn't realise and found it hard to accept that the only thing you can sponsor with a footballer is his boots!

We went to Moor Park several times and I was invited to play pro-am golf with Gary Player. That was definitely more their scene. They were nice people . . . but it became increasingly obvious to me they were a world away from football and everything I knew. Mark McCormack, though, was the closest I ever came to having an agent.

I don't begrudge an agent his percentage. If one of them comes to me with a proposition or a deal that looks legitimate and can earn for me, I don't mind. They are fully entitled to take their 20 per cent because it is money I wouldn't otherwise have had. But with most of them I would question just how loyal and sincere they are to their clients.

If I were a manager I would definitely be very careful about any dealings I had with the percentage men. League and UEFA rules state they are not allowed to play a part in transfer deals. But we all know they do . . . and usually get well looked after in the process.

Agents, however, are a part of the game now. They won't go away. You have got to accept them . . . and deal only with the good ones. One thing that has always irked me is the way they get involved in Cup final pools. Because the agent dictates whom you can and cannot talk to, there is nearly always aggravation. For what you get out of a pool after the taxman has taken his share, it is really not worth the trouble. It has upset me in the past when an agent has told me I cannot speak to a certain reporter because his newspaper has not put money in the pool. I think Pressmen will generally agree that I never duck and dive. They know where I am and if I can help, I will. Reporters have a job to do and I appreciate that.

Agents, hustlers, hangers-on, pop stars, politicians, millionaires . . . I have met the lot. I have travelled the world . . . North America, Central America, South America, Australia and the Far East, the Caribbean, Europe, East and West . . . more countries than I care to remember. Most I enjoyed, some I have absolutely no wish to see again. Football has opened a lot of doors . . . often of the best hotels at the cheapest prices. Football has taught me that who you know is as important as what you know.

I had two dreams as a kid. One was to be a professional footballer. The other was to be a pilot. One came true. The nearest I have got to the other is to sit up on the flight deck alongside the man flying the plane. Even that little privilege only came about because I was an Arsenal player!

I have had suits of the best cloth made for nothing and been given expensive gifts in different and exotic parts of the world. I met my wife Joy through football. We've got two smashing kids and above all I have known real happiness.

Truthfully, I have never taken for granted the advantages football has given me. The same as I have never taken for granted that my place at Arsenal is automatic. For the past two seasons I feel I have been at my best without any serious opposition to Tony Adams or myself. Now Steve Bould has arrived from Stoke and it is keeping both Tony and me on our toes. I have appreciated everything that has come my way through football – and I know I owe Arsenal Football Club so much. I have enjoyed every minute of my career. If it all ends tomorrow, the memories will last for ever.

This was David O'Leary's Arsenal record at the start of the 1988–89 season . . .

	Games	Goals
Football League	441	9
FA Cup	54	1
Littlewoods, Milk and League Cup	62	1
European Cup Winners' Cup	9	–
UEFA Cup	11	–
FA Charity Shield	1	–
Senior Friendlies	55	1
Overseas Tour Games	26	–
London Combination	44	2
SE Counties League	28	–
SE Counties League Cup	4	–
Junior Friendlies	13	2
Youth Tournaments	15	2
FA Youth Cup	4	–
S Junior Floodlight Cup	2	–